BECOMING UNSTACKABLE

Dark Power, Stacking, and the AI Revolution in Academic Governance

Ali Ayoub, Ph.D.

ALI AYOUB

Becoming Unstackable

Dark Power, Stacking, and the AI Revolution in Academic Governance

*To my beloved country, the United States of America —
the land that taught me the meaning of opportunity and the value
of freedom.
And to those who keep watch in the night so that others may live in
the light.*

*For the ghost contributors.
For those whose names were deleted from the slide.
For the future free thinkers who will rewrite the rules.
And for those who were told their independence was a flaw.*

Contents

Preface

Every year, thousands of the world's brightest minds disappear.

They do not vanish from the physical world. They disappear from the intellectual record. They are erased not by failure, incompetence, or a lack of work ethic, but by the very systems designed to cultivate them. They enter the academy as architects of the future; they leave as technicians of someone else's legacy, or they do not leave at all, trapped in a cycle of dependency that consumes their prime years.

This phenomenon is not unique to a specific university, a single country, or a particular field of study. I have seen it in the ivy-covered halls of the American Northeast, where prestige is the weapon of choice. I have tracked it through the hierarchical laboratories of East Asia, where cultural deference is weaponized to ensure silence. I have witnessed it in the under-resourced universities of the Global South, where access to a visa or a microscope is traded for absolute submission.

The pain is universal, but until now, it has been nameless. We call it "politics." We call it "paying your dues." We call it "bad mentorship." But these terms are too small. They imply that the problem is accidental—a matter of bad luck or difficult personalities.

It is not accidental. It is structural. And it is engineered.

This book gives that structure a name: **Stacking**.

Stacking is the invisible architecture of sabotage in academic governance. It is the systematic process by which institutions and gatekeepers actively suppress independent talent to maintain control. It operates through selective elevation, promoting those who offer compliant loyalty, and subtle isolation, erasing those who threaten the status quo with their autonomy.

At the heart of stacking lies a mechanism I have termed the **Trafficking of Attribution**.

To be clear: this term is not a metaphor for the profound human rights atrocities of physical human trafficking. It does not claim equivalence with bodily enslavement. Rather, it identifies a specific, professional form of capture that mimics those dynamics within the intellectual economy.

In academia, your name is your currency. Your attribution is your property. When a gatekeeper systematically harvests your ideas, your data, and your future potential while erasing your credit to feed their own survival, they are trafficking your intellectual capital. They are capturing your mind to service their debt to the system.

I wrote this book because I believe we are at a breaking point. The "Old Deal" of academia—*you give us your loyalty; we give you a career*—has collapsed. In its place is a hyper-competitive, scarcity-driven machine that incentives narcissism and punishes the very independence that drives discovery.

But this is not a book about despair. It is a manual for sovereignty.

In the pages that follow, you will meet Alex Reed. Alex is not a single person; Alex is a composite of the hundreds of researchers, students, interns and faculty I have interviewed and observed. Alex's story—from the seduction of being "chosen" to the shock of erasure, and finally to the clarity of reclaiming power—runs parallel to the analysis. It is there to remind us that while the systems are abstract, the cost is always human.

We will dissect the psychology of the "Stacker"—not to demonize them, but to understand the insecurities that drive them. We will map the "Global Variants" of this machine, from the prestige economies of the West to the enclave feudalism of the East. And, crucially, we will look to the future. We will explore how the "Unstackable" mindset, combined with the ethical application of Artificial Intelligence, can finally dismantle the shadows where these practices thrive.

You do not need the system's permission to be a free thinker. You never did. The labyrinth is vast, but it is not infinite. We are drawing the map.

Let us begin.

1

Chapter 1

DEFINING STACKING

The Invisible Architecture of Sabotage

1. The Vignette — The Phantom Exclusion

The first time it happened, Alex Reed didn't even know it was a "moment." It didn't arrive with the crash of a closing door or the sharp sting of an insult. It arrived in silence, on a Tuesday afternoon in early October, in a room that smelled faintly of dry-erase markers and ozone.

The lab was humming with its usual low-frequency vibration—the drone of the ultra-low freezers, the rhythmic click of pipettes, the murmur of ambitious students jockeying for bench space. Alex sat at the corner desk, finalizing the data set for the upcoming group meeting. This was the quarterly review, the high-stakes theater where Dr. Voss would parade his "star team" before the department chair to secure the renewal of the core grant.

For three months, Alex had lived inside the machinery of this project. It had been tedious, unglamorous work—calibrating the new sequencer until eyes blurred, rewriting the buggy analysis code line by line, running the negative controls that everyone else found too boring to touch. But it was the backbone. Without Alex's fix, the data was just noise. With it, the data was a breakthrough.

"Alright everyone, huddle up," Dr. Voss called out, clapping his hands with the performative energy of a coach rallying a team.

They gathered in the glass-walled conference room. Voss stood at the front, flanked by Maya and David, his two senior postdocs. They stood close to him, a subtle physical alignment that spoke of an inner circle already formed.

"I want to walk through the presentation deck for tomorrow," Voss said, dimming the lights. "We need to show the Chair that we are owning this field. No ambiguity. Pure dominance."

The projector hummed to life. The title slide flashed up in bold, sans-serif confidence: **Novel Mechanisms of Structural Dynamics.** Below it, the author list glowed in white against the dark background: **H. Voss, M. Chen, D. Evans.**

Alex blinked, waiting for the rest of the text to load. But the slide remained static. The name *Reed* was missing.

Before the shock could fully register, Voss clicked to the next slide. It was the optimization data. Alex's data. The graph Alex had generated at 2:00 AM on a Sunday, fueled by stale coffee and obsession, was now projected in high definition on the wall. The error bars were tight. The trend line was undeniable. It was beautiful work.

"As you can see," Voss said, his voice smooth and commanding, "Maya and David have managed to stabilize the signal-to-noise ratio. This optimization is the key to the whole grant renewal. It proves our hypothesis isn't just luck."

Maya nodded, jotting a note on her pad. David leaned back, crossing his arms, looking satisfied with a problem he hadn't solved.

A cold flush started at the base of Alex's neck. *Wait,* the internal voice whispered. *Maya didn't stabilize the signal. She was at a conference in Zurich that week. David doesn't even know how to run the Python script that generated this graph. I taught him the syntax.*

Alex raised a hand, tentatively at first, then higher. "Dr. Voss?"

Voss didn't stop speaking. He didn't even turn. He simply adjusted his stance, angling his body slightly so that his shoulder blocked Alex from the direct line of sight of the room. It was a subtle, physical wall—a gesture so small it could be called accidental, yet so precise it felt choreographed.

"We need to make sure the narrative is clean," Voss continued, addressing Maya directly, bypassing the raised hand in his periphery. "The Chair doesn't need to get bogged down in the technical weeds. Let's focus on the big picture implications. The story is what sells."

Voss glanced at his phone, which had been buzzing silently on the table—a message from a "former student" now high up at GenTech. He wasn't just managing the Chair; he was already seeding the narrative with the industry partners who would fund the next grant cycle. The data in front of us was just raw material; the real product was the story he was already selling to buyers we didn't even know existed.

Technical weeds.

The phrase hung in the air, landing with the weight of a verdict. In two words, Voss had redefined three months of intellectual architecture as janitorial work. He hadn't just stolen the credit; he had categorized the contribution as beneath notice. He had taken the foundation Alex built and treated it as dirt under the floorboards—necessary, perhaps, but meant to be walked upon, not seen.

The meeting moved on. Alex lowered their hand. The room felt suddenly smaller, the air thinner, as if the oxygen was being consumed by the people whose names were on the screen. No one looked at Alex. It wasn't that the others were being hostile; it was worse. They were being indifferent. The reality of the room had been set by the person with the most power, and in that reality, Alex Reed was a ghost.

Alex looked down at the notebook, at the pages of code and calculations that proved ownership. They were real. The ink was still fresh. But in this room, they didn't exist.

That evening, walking home under the gray autumn sky, Alex tried to rationalize it. The mind scrambled for a safe explanation. *Maybe it was a draft slide. Maybe there's a limit on author names for the internal update. Maybe I'm being oversensitive. Voss said we're a team. He calls us a family.*

But deep in the gut, the first fracture had appeared. Alex had walked into that room believing that merit was a currency—that if you did the work, you bought your place at the table. They walked out realizing that merit was merely a raw material—something to be harvested by those who owned the factory.

This was not an error. It was the system working exactly as designed.

2. Analysis — What is Stacking?

What happened to Alex in that conference room is the fundamental atomic unit of the phenomenon this book explores. To the untrained eye, the scene looks like a mundane instance of bad management—a busy professor forgetting a name, a chaotic slide deck, a moment of thoughtlessness. But forensic analysis reveals a different story.

This was not an oversight. It was an architecture.

Stacking is the strategic manipulation of visibility and opportunity within a hierarchy to maintain control. It is the invisible process by which institutions and gatekeepers actively suppress independent talent while systematically elevating those who offer compliant loyalty. It is a mechanism of governance that has infected academia from the Ivy League to the research hubs of Asia and the Global South.

When we strip away the academic politeness, Stacking reveals itself as a rigged game, operating on a set of unwritten but ruthlessly enforced laws.

The first of these is the law of **Selective Elevation**. A gatekeeper like Dr. Voss does not suppress everyone; if he did, his lab would collapse, and his grants would dry up. Instead, he engages in a careful curation of status. He chooses specific individuals—like Maya and David—to receive credit, visibility, and "ownership" of the collective output. These individuals are not necessarily the most talented, nor the most hardworking. They are simply the most *aligned*. They are the ones who reflect the Stacker's glory back to him, who do not challenge his narrative, and whose dependence on him is absolute. By elevating them, he creates a "Loyalty Class" that effectively polices the rest of the group. Alex is not just fighting Voss; Alex is fighting the consensus of the room.

But how is this theft justified? This brings us to the second mechanism: **Benevolent Erasure**.

Notice the language Voss used when he dismissed the "technical weeds." He did not say, "I am stealing Alex's work." He said, "I am streamlining the story." This is the genius of the Stacker. They frame the exclusion of the independent thinker not as malice, but as a necessary act of leadership. They are protecting the narrative. They are focusing on the big picture. They are saving the Department Chair from boredom.

This framing allows the Stacker to strip-mine intellectual capital while maintaining the moral high ground. To the outsider, Voss looks like a focused, pragmatic leader making tough executive decisions. To the victim, however, the message is devastatingly clear: *Your work is valuable, but you are not.* The theft is hidden behind the veil of administrative necessity.

Finally, Stacking relies on the accumulation of **Invisible Walls**.

When Alex raised a hand, there was no shouting match. There was no dramatic confrontation that could be reported to Human Resources. There was simply a turned shoulder. Stacking rarely involves screaming. Instead, it thrives on micro-exclusions: the meeting invite that was "accidentally" forgotten; the email reply that never comes; the physical blocking of a line of sight; the conversation that goes silent when you enter the room.

Individually, these moments are trivial. They are easily denied. If Alex were to complain, Voss could simply say, "I didn't see you," or "We were just short on time." But cumulatively, they build a prison. They send a binary signal to the brain, repeated day after day until it becomes a belief: *You do not belong here.*

We use the term "Stacking" because the mechanism resembles the stacking of a deck of cards in a gambling hall. The "house"—the institution or the gatekeeper—arranges the order of the deck so that no matter how well you play your hand, the outcome is predetermined. They stack the **Credit**, top-loading it to themselves and the inner circle. They stack the **Labor**, bottom-loading the difficult, invisible work to the independents. And they stack the **Narrative**, ensuring that the history of the discovery is written only by the victors.

For the independent thinker, this creates a profound cognitive dissonance. You are doing the work, but you are not seeing the return. You are feeding the machine, but the machine is starving you. You begin to question your own sanity. *Am I invisible?* you ask. *Am I failing?*

The answer is no. You are not failing. You are being Stacked. The invisible architecture has been built around you, and for the first time, you are seeing the walls. And as we will discover in the chapters to come, once you can see the walls, you can begin to dismantle them.

2

Chapter 2

THE ROOTS OF INSTITUTIONAL NARCISSISM

Why the System Rewards the Self-Obsessed

1. The Vignette — The Shrine of the Mirror

The second week of the rotation, Alex was summoned to Dr. Voss's office for a one-on-one strategy session. The email had been brief—*"Come by at 4. We need to align on the vision."*—but the word *vision* sent a flicker of anticipation through Alex's chest. In a world of technical details, the promise of a "vision" felt like an invitation to the inner sanctum.

Voss's office was not merely a workspace; it was a cathedral to his own curriculum vitae. The walls were lined not with books, but with framed artifacts of conquest: glossy covers of *Nature* and *Cell* featuring his name in bold type; awards from societies in Geneva and Tokyo gleaming on backlit shelves; a large, black-and-white photograph of Voss shaking hands with

8

a Nobel laureate, both men laughing as if they shared a private joke the rest of the world wasn't smart enough to understand.

Alex sat in the low leather chair across from the massive mahogany desk. The positioning was deliberate. Voss sat higher, backlit by the window, his face in shadow while the afternoon sun illuminated Alex fully. It was an interrogation setup disguised as a chat.

"I see a lot of myself in you, Alex," Voss began, leaning back and tenting his fingers.

The compliment landed with the precision of a dart. It was flattering, yes, but it was also a command. *Be like me.*

"Most students," Voss continued, his voice dropping to a confidential register, "come here wanting a degree. They want a job. They want security. They are... pedestrians." He waved a hand dismissively at the door, as if the hallway outside were filled with disappointment. "I am not interested in pedestrians. I am interested in legacy. I am building something that will last fifty years after I am gone. The question is: are you here to do science, or are you here to build history with me?"

Alex nodded, entranced. "I want to do work that matters."

"Good," Voss smiled. It was a warm, expansive smile that felt like sunlight breaking through clouds. "Because the work we do here is dangerous. The establishment hates us. They hate us because we move too fast. We ask the questions they are too afraid to ask. That is why I need total alignment. When the arrows start flying, I need to know you are standing in the shield wall with me, not looking for the exit."

He stood up and walked to the wall of framed covers, tracing a finger along the glass of a *Science* paper from 2018.

"Maya understands this," he said, not turning around. "She knows that my name on a paper opens doors that would otherwise remain locked forever. She understands that her success is a subset of my success. That is why she will go far."

He turned back to Alex, the warmth suddenly cooler, the eyes searching. "I need to know if you understand that too. You have a brilliant mind, Alex. I can see the gears turning. But brilliance without loyalty is just noise. Are you ready to be part of the signal?"

In that moment, Alex felt a rush of gratitude so intense it masked the warning bells ringing in the distance. Voss wasn't just offering mentorship; he was offering membership in an elite tribe. He was offering protection from the "pedestrians."

"I am," Alex said. "I'm ready."

"Excellent." Voss sat down, the interview over as abruptly as it had begun. "Then cancel your weekend plans. The grant deadline is Monday, and we need to rewrite the preliminary data section to fit the new narrative. Welcome to the team."

Alex walked out of the office feeling taller, heavier with purpose. It would take months to realize what had actually happened in that room. Voss hadn't been interviewing a student; he had been recruiting a mirror. He didn't want a colleague. He wanted a reflection.

The "vision" wasn't about science. It was about Voss. And Alex had just volunteered to be the glass.

2. Analysis — The Architecture of Ego

If we analyze the interaction in Voss's office, we see the blueprint of **Institutional Narcissism**.

This term does not simply refer to a professor who has a big ego. In academia, big egos are common currency. **Institutional Narcissism** is something more specific and more toxic: it is a systemic adaptation where the institution itself selects, rewards, and protects individuals who exhibit narcissistic traits, turning those traits into professional virtues.

Dr. Voss is not an anomaly. He is the archetype of the modern "Star Professor." And to understand why Stacking happens, we must understand the three pillars that hold up his world.

a. The Cult of the Genius Academia is one of the last professional sectors that explicitly worships the "Great Man" theory of history. We are taught that discovery is the product of solitary genius—the Einstein, the Darwin, the Curie. Voss leverages this myth perfectly. His office is a shrine to his own "genius," designed to intimidate and awe. By framing himself as a visionary fighting against "pedestrians" and "the establishment," he creates a reality distortion field.

- **The Trap:** If Voss is a singular genius, then normal rules don't apply to him. He doesn't need to follow HR policies; he is "disrupting the field." He doesn't need to be fair; he needs to be "great."
- **The Impact:** Alex accepts the abuse (working weekends, erasing self) because it is framed as the price of admission to greatness.

b. The Supply Chain of Admiration Psychologically, a narcissist requires a constant stream of what is known as **Narcissistic Supply**—admiration, validation, and confirmation of their superiority. In a university, graduate students and postdocs are the perfect supply chain. They are dependent, they are structurally inferior, and they are eager to please. When Voss says, *"I see a lot of myself in you,"* he is not complimenting Alex. He is attempting to clone himself. He is testing whether Alex is capable of providing that supply.

- **The Test:** Will Alex reflect Voss's glory?
- **The Result:** Maya (the "Loyalty Class") has passed the test by accepting that her success is a "subset" of his. She has agreed to be a supply source. Alex is being groomed to do the same.

c. The Institutional Shield Why does the university allow Voss to operate like a feudal lord? Because the institution itself is narcissistic. Modern universities are obsessed with rankings, prestige, grant dollars, and "star power." Voss brings in the grants. Voss gets the covers of *Nature*. Voss raises the university's h-index. Therefore, the institution incentivizes his behavior.

- **The Incentive:** If Voss extracts labor from students to pump up his publication record, the university rewards him with tenure and chairs.
- **The Blind Eye:** If a student complains, the institution calculates the cost. Losing Voss costs millions in grant money. Losing a student costs nothing. The system does not just tolerate the narcissist; it requires him. He is the engine of the prestige economy.

The "Narcissistic Contract" In that office, Voss offered Alex a contract that is invisible to lawyers but binding in blood: *I will let you be near my power, and in exchange, you will give me your identity.*

This is the root of Stacking. Stacking is simply the mechanism the narcissist uses to manage his supply chain. He elevates those who mirror him (Maya), and he erases those who threaten to shine on their own (Alex).

It is not personal. It is metabolic. The narcissist must consume to survive, and the independent thinker is the one thing he cannot digest.

3

Chapter 3

PSYCHOLOGICAL MECHANISMS OF CONTROL

How the System Breaks the Will

1. The Vignette — The Reality Distortion Field

By November, the lab had acquired a new texture for Alex. It was no longer a place of discovery; it was a minefield where the map changed daily.

The crisis arrived on a Thursday morning. Alex had spent the previous week running the "Protocol B" series—a high-risk, high-reward set of experiments that Voss had explicitly requested during their last one-on-one. Voss had been adamant, leaning over the mahogany desk, eyes bright with intensity: *"Drop the standard controls, Alex. They're a waste of reagents. Go straight for the B-series. We need to beat the Geneva group to this data."*

Alex had hesitated—skipping controls was risky—but Voss's

confidence was a force of nature. *"Trust me,"* he had said. *"I know where the gold is."*

So Alex ran the B-series. It was a grueling 80-hour week, fueled by vending machine coffee and anxiety. But the results came in, and they were spectacular. The signal was clean. The hypothesis held.

Alex walked into the weekly data meeting with a rare sense of safety. The data was printed, the slides were ready, the directive had been followed to the letter.

Voss sat at the head of the table, scrolling through his phone. He didn't look up as Alex began presenting.

"As you requested," Alex said, "I focused exclusively on the Protocol B series this week. Here are the primary reads."

Voss stopped scrolling. The room went silent. He looked up, his expression one of baffled disappointment.

"Protocol B?" Voss asked, his voice quiet, dangerous. "Why would you run Protocol B without the standard controls? That's scientifically illiterate."

Alex froze. The air left the room. "Because... you told me to. Last Tuesday. In your office. You said the controls were a waste of reagents and to beat the Geneva group."

Voss let out a short, incredulous laugh. He looked at Maya, then at David, inviting them into the joke. "Alex, I would never say that. That violates basic experimental design. Why would I tell you to sabotage your own data?"

"You said—" Alex started, but the certainty was already crumbling. *Did he?* The memory was vivid—the sunlight on the desk, the leaning forward, the specific phrase about the Geneva group. But Voss's conviction was absolute. He didn't look like a liar; he looked like a disappointed mentor dealing with a confused student.

"I think you're confused," Voss said, his tone softening to a pitying gentleness that was far worse than anger. "You're under a lot of pressure. Sometimes we hear what we want to hear. But this... this is unusable. You've wasted a week."

He turned to Maya. "Maya, can you take over the C-series? We need someone reliable on this."

Alex sat down, the blood rushing in their ears. The notebook in front of them felt heavy, useless. *I heard him,* Alex thought. *I know I heard him.* But looking around the room, seeing the averted eyes of the other students, the doubt took root. *Maybe I did misunderstand. Maybe I am cracking.*

Later that afternoon, as Alex was cleaning the bench, numb with shame, Voss walked by. He stopped, placing a hand on Alex's shoulder.

"Don't beat yourself up," Voss said warmly, his voice back to the 'Architect' persona of Chapter 2. "I push you because you have greatness in you, Alex. I just need you to be sharper. Get some rest. We'll try again Monday."

The warmth was intoxicating. The shame evaporated, replaced by a desperate surge of gratitude. *He doesn't hate me,* Alex thought. *He still believes in me. I just need to be better.*

Alex went home that night determined to work harder, to listen better, to be worthy of the forgiveness. They didn't realize that the crisis had been manufactured. The confusion was the point. The forgiveness was the hook.

Alex wasn't being mentored. They were being conditioned.

2. The Toolkit of Control

The interaction in the conference room was not a miscommunication. It was a deployment of specific, military-grade psychological weapons designed to erode autonomy. Dr. Voss is not just a "bad boss"; he is a practitioner of coercive control.

To understand Stacking, we must dissect the toolkit. These mechanisms are used to keep the independent thinker off-balance, dependent, and silent.

a. Gaslighting: The Distortion of Reality. Gaslighting is the systematic denial of reality to cause the victim to doubt their own memory and sanity. When Voss denied giving the instruction, he wasn't just covering his tracks; he was destabilizing Alex's cognitive baseline. By doing it publicly, he enlisted the group (social proof) to validate his version of reality.

- **The Goal:** To make Alex trust Voss's reality more than their own perceptions.
- **The Result:** Next time, Alex will not trust their own judgment. They will check with Voss for everything. Independence dies; dependency is born.

b. Intermittent Reinforcement: The Addiction Machine. This is the most powerful weapon in the Stacker's arsenal. In psychology, this is known as the "Slot Machine Effect." If Voss were abusive 100% of the time, Alex would quit. If he were kind 100% of the time, Alex would be secure. Instead, Voss delivers pain (public humiliation) followed unpredictably by pleasure (warmth, "I believe in you").

- **The Psychology:** The brain releases more dopamine in anticipation of an *uncertain* reward than a guaranteed one.
- **The Trap:** Alex stays not because it is good, but because they are addicted to the moments when the abuse stops. They work harder and harder to trigger the "jackpot" of Voss's approval.

c. Isolation and the "Social Freeze". Stacking work best in the dark. The Stacker actively prevents the target from comparing notes with others.

- **Triangulation:** Voss gives the C-series to Maya right in front of Alex. This creates rivalry. Alex now views Maya as a threat, not an ally. Maya views Alex as incompetent. They will never talk honestly. The labor force is divided.
- **The Freeze:** When a target is marked as "confused" or "difficult," the group instinctively distances themselves to avoid becoming collateral damage. Alex stops getting invited to lunch. The isolation chamber is sealed.

d. The Double Bind: Voss places Alex in a situation where every choice is wrong.

- **Choice A:** Follow the instruction (Run Protocol B). *Result: Humiliation for being "scientifically illiterate."*
- **Choice B:** Ignore the instruction (Run Controls). *Result: Humiliation for "not listening" or being risk-averse.* The Double Bind creates a state of "learned helplessness." The victim stops acting to avoid punishment, becoming entirely passive and malleable.

e. Weaponized Bureaucracy (The Scarcity Trap): While not shown in this specific vignette, a common companion to these psychological tactics is administrative sabotage.

- "Lost" paperwork that delays a degree.
- Funding that is "pending" forever.
- Deadlines that shift without notice. This keeps the target

in a state of survival mode. When you are fighting for your basic resources (visa, stipend, graduation timeline), you do not have the energy to fight for your intellectual rights.

The Dark Economy These mechanisms create a closed economy within the lab.

- **The Currency:** Voss's mood.
- **The Tax:** Your self-esteem.
- **The Product:** Your compliance.

Alex believes the problem is their own "confusion." But the confusion is external. It is a generated fog of war. And until Alex realizes that the fog is artificial, they will never find the exit.

3. Sidebar — The Global Variants of Control

Stacking does not look the same everywhere.

It adapts to its ecosystem like a psychological parasite, evolving new strategies depending on the cultural soil in which it grows.

In the powerful universities of the US, UK, and Western Europe, a particular variant flourishes — the **Prestige Stacker**. These are the masters of polished cruelty, cloaking exploitation behind the immaculate language of professionalism. Nothing is openly hostile; everything is "procedural." Gaslighting becomes "performance management." Exclusion becomes "fit." And because lawsuits lurk in the shadows of every departmental meeting, these stackers leave no trace. Their power lies in what is never written down — the "off the record" conversation, the missing email, the handshake that determines a future without ever appearing on paper. In this ecosystem, the only vulnerability is documentation. Shine light on the whispers, and their kingdom trembles.

In high power-distance cultures — across parts of Asia, the Middle East, and other lineage-based academic traditions — a different variant rules: the **Filial Stacker**. Here, authority is not simply institutional; it is parental. The professor does not position themselves as a supervisor, but as a patriarch or matriarch of an academic "family." Independence is reframed as disrespect. Questioning becomes ingratitude. The fear is no longer professional failure but moral exile — a total removal from the social and intellectual lineage. Once cast out, the student is not just academically stranded; they are spiritually disowned. And yet this variant has its weakness: face. When external success bypasses the "parent," it shatters the illusion of absolute authority.

In under-resourced regions — from parts of the Global South to universities with chronic funding scarcity — the Stacker mutates again into the **Resource Stacker**. Here, power is distilled to its rawest form: access. The gatekeeper controls the only visa-granting letter, the only microscope that works, the only connection to international collaborators. This variant does not need to raise its voice; it simply has to close a door. If you leave, you lose your future. If you stay, you owe your life. Their control is total — until someone builds a digital bridge that bypasses them entirely. For this variant, the only antidote is sovereignty through global connection.

4

Chapter 4

THE TRAFFICKING OF ATTRIBUTION

Capturing Minds and Intellectual Capital

1. The Vignette — The Theft of the Future

Three months into the new year, the "Protocol B" data—the data Alex had generated during that feverish eighty-hour week—had grown into a manuscript. It was a solid paper, perhaps even a great one. The story was tight, the figures were clean, and the implications for the field were undeniable.

Alex had written the Methods section and drafted the primary results. It was the first time Alex felt a true sense of ownership. The confusion of the "gaslighting" incident in Chapter 3 had faded, replaced by the tangible weight of a finished PDF file. *This is why I'm here*, Alex thought. *The work speaks.*

The email from Dr. Voss arrived at 10:00 PM on a Friday. *"Team, the manuscript is ready for submission to Nature Comm.*

Review the attached final draft. We submit Monday morning."

Alex opened the file, heart racing with the specific adrenaline of a young scientist about to see their name in print. The title page loaded.

Mechanisms of Structural Dynamics in Protein Folding Authors: H. Voss, M. Chen, D. Evans, S. Patel, J. Kim, A. Reed.

Alex stared at the screen. The air in the apartment seemed to stop moving. *Sixth.* Alex was the sixth author.

Maya (M. Chen) was second. David (D. Evans) was third. Two other postdocs who had barely touched the project were fourth and fifth. Alex—who had redesigned the protocol, debugged the code, and generated the pivotal Figure 2—was listed last, just before the senior author slot. In some fields, the last slot is prestigious. In this field, for a student, it was the "technician" slot. It meant: *This person washed the beakers.*

The authorship order didn't tell the story of the discovery. It told the story of the hierarchy.

Alex waited until Monday morning, standing outside Voss's office door, rehearsing the sentences to keep the voice from shaking. When the door opened, Voss looked up, smiling that same warm, dangerous smile.

"Alex! Did you see the draft? It's a beauty, isn't it?"

"I did," Alex said, stepping inside and closing the door. "It looks great. But I wanted to ask about the author list. The protocol redesign... that was my work. Figure 2 is my data. I thought... I expected to be higher than sixth."

Voss's smile didn't drop, but the temperature in the room plummeted. He sighed, taking off his glasses, adopting the weary expression of a parent explaining gravity to a toddler.

"Alex, authorship is a complex calculus. It's not just about who pipetted the liquid. It's about *intellectual lineage.* Maya held the conceptual framework for this project long before you joined. David provided the grant support. The others... well, they need this publication for their fellowship renewals next month. You're just starting. You have time."

"But the work—" Alex started.

"The work is important," Voss interrupted, his voice hardening. "And you are on the paper. That is generous. Many labs wouldn't include a rotation student at all. This is a gift, Alex. Be grateful you're on the board."

He put his glasses back on, signaling the end of the audience. "Focus on being a team player. If you fight for scraps now, you'll starve later. If you help the team eat, eventually, you'll get a seat at the head of the table."

Alex left the office feeling hollowed out. It wasn't just that the credit was wrong. It was the logic. Voss had just admitted that the authorship wasn't a record of contribution; it was a currency. He was using Alex's labor to buy David's fellowship. He was using Alex's data to bolster Maya's career.

Alex walked back to the bench, looked at the pipette, and realized for the first time that they were not an architect of discovery. They were a battery. Voss was draining the energy from one source and pouring it into another, ensuring that the lights stayed on in the places he chose to illuminate.

The work remained. But the future it should have bought—the citations, the reputation, the career capital—had been trafficked away.

2. Analysis — Defining the Crime

What Dr. Voss committed in that office is the core mechanism of the system. It is not merely "unfair." It is the **Trafficking of Attribution**.

To understand this concept, we must first make a crucial distinction. **Disclaimer:** *The term "trafficking" is used here in its professional and economic sense—the illicit trade and movement of goods or capital. It is not an analogy to the human rights atrocities of sex trafficking or modern slavery. We do not conflate professional theft with bodily violation. However, the psychological mechanism—the grooming, the capture, and the exploitation of vulnerability—bears a structural resemblance that warrants the severity of the language.*

What is the Trafficking of Attribution? It is the systematic capture, redirection, and appropriation of **Intellectual Capital**—ideas, data, credit, and future potential—from vulnerable producers (students/independents) to serve the interests of gatekeepers and their chosen networks.

In the academic economy, **Attribution is Currency**.

- A salary pays your rent.
- Attribution (authorship, citations, reputation) pays for your *career*. When Voss moves Alex from 2nd author to 6th, he is not hurting Alex's feelings. He is stealing Alex's future. He is taking the currency Alex earned and depositing it into Maya's account.

The Lifecycle of the Trade This trafficking operates through a predictable lifecycle, which we can now map onto Alex's journey:

a. The Selection (The Profile). The Stacker identifies a target who produces high-value work but lacks political cover. Alex was perfect: talented, hardworking, but naive about the "game."

b. The Hook (The Debt). Recall Chapter 6 (The Love Bomb). Voss told Alex, *"I will give you the world."* He created a sense of indebtedness. Alex felt "lucky" just to be in the room. This perceived debt is used to justify the theft later. *"This authorship is a gift,"* Voss said, implying Alex should pay *him* for the privilege of being robbed.

c. The Capture (The Harvest) The work is done. The data is generated. Once the intellectual capital exists, the Stacker seizes control of it. The narrative is rewritten. *"Maya held the conceptual framework"* is code for *"Maya needs the credit more than you do, and she is loyal to me."*

d. The Redistribution (The Payout) The Stacker redistributes the stolen credit to maintain his power structure.

- He gives it to **Maya** to secure her loyalty and build her into a "star" who reflects his genius.
- He gives it to **David** to ensure his funding (fellowship) gets renewed, which keeps money flowing into the lab.
- He gives the scraps to **Alex** to keep them just hungry enough to stay, but not strong enough to leave.

Why It Remains Invisible This crime is almost impossible to prosecute because it relies on **Subjectivity**. There is no legal definition of "significant contribution." The International Committee of Medical Journal Editors (ICMJE) has guidelines, but no police force. If Alex complains to the Dean, Voss will simply say, *"In my professional judgment, Alex's contribution was technical, not intellectual."* The Dean will not read the Python code. The Dean will look at the grant dollars Voss brings in, and the case will be closed.

The "Ghost Contributor" The result of this trafficking is the creation of a class of **Ghost Contributors**—researchers whose ideas form the bedrock of their fields, but whose names appear only in the footnotes of history. They fuel the machine, but they do not steer it.

Alex left that office with a paycheck, but without the capital. Voss had successfully laundered the work. The data was now his.

5

Chapter 5

PROFILING THE STACKER

The Psychology of Dark Agendas and the Vampire Empire

1. The Vignette — The Voice Behind the Door

It was late in the semester, the time of year when the sun sets before five o'clock and the lab takes on a subterranean feel. Alex was working alone, finishing a long series of centrifugations. The rhythm of the work was hypnotic, a way to numb the stinging memory of the authorship meeting.

The hallway was quiet, save for the hum of the ventilation. As Alex walked past Dr. Voss's office to get more ice, the door was slightly ajar. Voss was inside, his back to the door, wearing a headset, speaking to a video monitor. He was laughing—a relaxed, genuine sound that Alex hadn't heard in months.

Alex slowed down. It wasn't intentional eavesdropping at first; it was just the instinct to gauge the weather. *Is he in a good mood? Is it safe to say hello?*

"No, no, the kid's bright, certainly," Voss said, his voice carrying clearly into the corridor. "But he's got this... independent streak. Keeps asking questions that slow the tempo. I run a tight ship, Marcus. I need people who row, not people who try to steer."

Alex froze, pressing back against the wall, heart hammering against the ribs.

"Maya is perfect for the renewal," Voss continued. "She executes. She doesn't second-guess the narrative. But this new one? Alex? I'll keep him busy with the support work until he either breaks in or burns out. Either way, the problem solves itself."

There was a pause as the person on the other end spoke. Then Voss laughed again, a soft, self-satisfied chuckle.

"It's not cruelty, Marcus. It's curation. The lab is my legacy. I decide who gets to be part of the history and who is just a footnote. If they can't serve the vision, they don't get the visibility."

Alex walked away, leaving the ice bucket behind. The fluorescent lights of the corridor felt suddenly harsh, exposing. For months, Alex had wondered if the exclusion was accidental—a byproduct of Voss being too busy, too stressed, too focused. Now, the truth was laid bare. Voss wasn't incompetent. He wasn't overwhelmed. He was *deliberate*. The stacking wasn't an accident; it was a strategy.

For the first time, the gatekeeper had a face. He wasn't a mentor failing at his job. He was an architect succeeding at his.

2. Analysis — The Taxonomy of Control

The Stacker is rarely a cartoon villain. Far more often, they are highly functional, outwardly successful academics—tenured, grant-funded, and widely admired. They have adapted to the hyper-competitive ecosystem of the university in a way that makes Stacking feel not only rational to them, but necessary. Profiling the Stacker is not an exercise in judgment; it is an exercise in demystification.

Through our research, we have identified four primary archetypes. However, there is a fifth, darker variant that operates not just within the university, but across the entire industry.

The Narcissist (The Mirror) sees students as extensions of themselves. They do not want distinct individuals; they want clones who reflect their genius. Their mechanism is love-bombing followed by devaluation.

The Machiavellian (The Strategist) views academia as a zero-sum game. They are transactionally invested in you. You are an asset to be maximized or a liability to be minimized. They hoard information and release it only to those who provide the highest return on investment.

The Legacy Builder (The Anxious Gatekeeper) fears obsoles-cence. They stack to hold their ground, erasing students who use methods the professor doesn't understand to avoid looking obsolete.

The Enclave Builder (The "Imported Absolutist") is increas-ingly common in globalized academia. They recruit almost exclusively from their country of origin, not for diversity, but for leverage. They know these students are doubly locked by visa dependence and cultural debt. They create a "Lab within a Lab," a feudal enclave where students trade their freedom for a chance at a life in a new country.

3. The Vampire Empire — The Corporate Spy Ring

There is a final, terrifying dimension to the Stacker's profile that is often invisible until it is too late. We call this **The Academic Cartel**.

This is not a new phenomenon; it is an operation that has been running for decades. The Narcissist does not just build a lab; they build an intelligence network. Over decades, they place their most loyal "Enclave" soldiers in key positions at major pharmaceutical companies, tech giants, and government agencies.

This creates a feedback loop of **Corporate Espionage**. The outbound flow consists of the professor placing loyalists in high-ranking industry jobs. But the inbound flow is where the illegality thrives. These "sleeper" alumni feed industry data, and emerging trends back to the professor. The professor then uses this insider information to write grants that miraculously "predict" industry shifts, file patents, or launch startups that align perfectly with future market needs.

In reality, it is an empire built on a continuous stream of illicit intelligence. The students in these companies are not just alumni; they are assets. And crucially, they are **enforcers**.

If a victim like Alex tries to escape by applying for a job at one of these companies, the "sleeper" receives the application. They contact the Stacker. The application is flagged and rejected—not based on merit, but on the Stacker's order. The network ensures that the Stacker's control extends far beyond the campus gates. It is a roadmap of vicious narcissism that turns the entire industry into a minefield for the independent thinker.

6

Chapter 6

ENTERING THE LABYRINTH

The Trap of Being Chosen

1. The Vignette — The Architect Speech

The email from Dr. Voss had arrived two weeks before the semester even started, a digital summons that felt less like an administrative notice and more like a royal decree. It wasn't a form letter sent to the entire cohort. It was personal, specific, and flattering. *"Alex, I've been reviewing the incoming files, and your background in computational modeling is exactly the missing piece my lab needs. Let's meet before orientation. I want to hear your vision."*

Alex sat in Voss's office that first morning, the September sun warming the spine of the high-backed leather guest chair. The room was a monument to influence, lined with shelves that held not just books, but artifacts of conquest: awards from societies in Geneva and Tokyo, photos with Nobel laureates, and the glossy covers of journals that defined the field.

Voss didn't sit behind his massive mahogany desk. Instead, he pulled a chair around to sit facing Alex, leaning forward with his elbows on his knees, his eyes locked on Alex's face with intense, focused interest.

"The department is full of technicians," Voss said, his voice dropping to a conspiratorial whisper that made the large room feel intimate. "People who can run protocols but can't *think*. I saw your proposal on structural dynamics. It's raw, yes. But it's architectural. You see the system, not just the bricks."

He smiled—a warm, electric expression that made Alex feel like the only other intelligent person in the building. It was a heady sensation. After years of fighting to be taken seriously in undergraduate labs, here was a gatekeeper holding the door wide open.

"I'm building a legacy here, Alex," Voss continued. "I need a lieutenant, not just another pair of hands. Someone who can help me reshape the field. I think that could be you."

Alex felt a flush of pride so intense it was almost dizzying. The impostor syndrome that had plagued Alex for months evaporated under the heat of Voss's attention.

"I'd be honored," Alex managed to say.

"Good." Voss stood up, clapping a hand on Alex's shoulder. "You'll start on the core grant immediately. It's high pressure, but I protect my own. You give me your loyalty, I give you the world. That's the deal."

Later that afternoon, the department held its welcome mixer in the atrium. Alex stood near the cheese platter with a plastic cup of cheap wine, feeling a secret weight of importance. While other students were nervously introducing themselves, Alex already had a mission.

Maya, a senior graduate student in Voss's lab, approached. She looked tired, her eyes scanning the room with a detached wariness.

"He took you for coffee?" she asked, her voice flat.

"Yes," Alex said, unable to suppress a smile. "We discussed the grant. He has some big ideas."

Maya nodded, looking down at her drink. "He calls it the 'Architect Speech.' He gave it to me four years ago. Just be careful what you sign up for, Alex. Being his favorite is more expensive than being ignored."

Alex brushed the comment aside, chalking it up to jealousy. Maya looked exhausted; perhaps she just wasn't keeping up with the pace Voss demanded. Voss had *seen* Alex. Voss had *chosen* Alex. The labyrinth didn't look like a trap from where Alex was standing. It looked like a fast lane.

Alex stepped in willingly, believing they had been handed the keys to the kingdom, not realizing they had just put on the handcuffs.

As Alex walked home, buzzing with the cheap wine and the high of the "Architect Speech," the phone rang. It was Mom. It was their Sunday ritual—a catch-up call that had anchored Alex through the chaos of undergrad.

Alex looked at the screen, then at the stack of grant papers Voss had handed over. *"I need total alignment,"* Voss had said.

For the first time, Alex hit 'Decline' and sent a quick text: *Can't talk, huge opportunity just landed. Working late.*

It felt like a small, necessary sacrifice for the sake of the career. Alex didn't realize it was the first brick in a wall that would eventually silence that phone entirely.

2. Analysis — The Mechanics of Seduction

The most dangerous stackers do not begin their relationship with abuse, neglect, or theft. If they did, their victims would simply leave. Instead, they begin with a psychological maneuver known as **Idealization**, or more colloquially, "Love Bombing." This phase serves a critical structural purpose in the architecture of control: it manufactures a debt of gratitude and secures the target's identity as an extension of the gatekeeper's ego.

When Voss separates Alex from the "technicians" and invites them into the fold of the "architects," he is deploying the **"Special Person" Narrative**. By framing the relationship as a partnership of geniuses against a world of mediocrity, Voss ensures that Alex will interpret future demands not as exploitation, but as the burden of greatness. This narrative acts as a powerful inoculant against dissent. If Alex later feels overworked or undervalued, the internal monologue will not be "My boss is exploitative," but rather "I must work harder to prove I am an architect, not a technician."

This dynamic relies heavily on the **Transaction of Loyalty**. In the vignette, Voss explicitly states the contract: *"You give me your loyalty, I give you the world."* To a young, ambitious researcher, this sounds like mentorship. In reality, it is a high-stakes purchase of the self. In organizational psychology, this establishes an immediate, high-intensity Leader-Member Exchange relationship, but one that is strictly conditional. The unspoken corollary of Voss's promise is terrifyingly simple: *The moment you withhold total loyalty, I will withhold the world.*

The seduction also serves a tactical function known as **Isolation via Elevation**. By telling Alex they are "better" than the others, Voss subtly cuts Alex off from their peers before the semester even begins. When Maya offers a warning, Alex views it through the lens Voss has already polished: Maya is just a "technician," or perhaps she is jealous of the new "lieutenant." This is preventative triangulation. By convincing the victim they are above the group, the stacker ensures the victim will never ally *with* the group against the leader. The victim becomes an island, accessible only by the stacker.

For independent thinkers, this phase is often described as the **Golden Handcuffs**. High-performing individuals are often not looking for a boss; they are looking for a champion. They crave intellectual validation and a space where their ideas are taken seriously. The stacker mimics this champion perfectly. They offer resources, access, and praise, creating a rush of dopamine that binds the target to them.

The tragedy of the labyrinth is that the entry is not forced. The victim enters feeling empowered, fueled by the rush of being chosen. They do not see the walls rising around them because they are too focused on the light shining from the gatekeeper's office.

But the bill always comes due. The "Architect Speech" was not a job offer; it was a grooming tactic. And as Alex will soon discover, the price of the "world" Voss promised is the erasure of the self.

3. Empowerment Insight — Recognizing the Rush

The first defense against this phase of Stacking is to recognize the emotional signature of the trap. Real mentorship builds slowly. It is based on shared work, mutual respect, and gradual trust. It is rarely established in a single meeting, and it almost never requires you to view your peers with contempt.

If you leave a first meeting feeling an intense, dizzying "rush" of validation—if you feel you have been anointed as the "chosen one" before you have even generated a single data point—you are likely being Love Bombed. This is a red flag, not a green light.

The strategy here is emotional sobriety. When a gatekeeper offers you the world in exchange for unspecified loyalty, do not accept the debt. Thank them for the opportunity, but keep your internal assets—your ideas, your trust, and your identity—liquid. Do not sign the psychological contract. Enter the lab if you must, but keep one foot in the hallway, and remember that anyone who tries to isolate you from your peers is not raising you up; they are merely clearing the space to tear you down.

7

Chapter 7

THE FIRST FRACTURES

Subtle Shifts and Early Isolation

1. The Vignette — The Narrowing Hallway

The rotation had officially ended, and Alex stayed on in Voss's lab, carried by the momentum of that initial promise. The "Architect Speech" still echoed in Alex's mind, a warm memory that buffered against the increasing coldness of the daily reality. The rhythm of the lab had settled into a grind: long hours running assays under the harsh glow of fume hood lights, quiet afternoons analyzing data on a flickering screen, and the weekly group meetings where Voss presided like a conductor, his voice echoing off the whiteboards.

Alex had learned to speak less and observe more. The questions still bubbled up, but they were timed carefully now—offered only after the senior postdocs had spoken, phrased as humble suggestions rather than intellectual challenges, always accompanied by a careful nod to Voss's prior work.

One Tuesday in late October, a ripple of excitement moved through the department atrium. A flyer had been posted for the upcoming "Emerging Scholars Symposium," a prestigious internal event with limited speaking slots. It was the kind of opportunity that launched careers—a chance to present to the Dean and visiting fellows.

Alex, eating lunch alone at a corner table, saw the flyer and felt a spark of ambition. The "Protocol B" data was solid. It was novel. It fits the theme perfectly. That afternoon, Alex drafted a short, rigorous abstract. It wasn't revolutionary, but it was clean science, built directly on the group's recent findings with a clever computational twist.

Alex attached the draft to an email to Voss with a polite, hopeful note: *"Dr. Voss, I thought this might fit the symposium theme. I'd love to represent the lab. Happy to discuss."*

No reply came that day. Or the next.

On Thursday, during the weekly lab meeting, the room smelled of stale coffee and dry-erase markers. Voss stood at the front, scrolling through the agenda. When he reached the "Announcements" section, he smiled—that familiar, winning smile that made everyone lean in.

"I'm pleased to announce our lineup for the Emerging Scholars Symposium," Voss said. "Maya will be presenting the keynote for our group, showcasing the structural dynamics project. And David has secured a lightning talk slot."

The room erupted in a murmur of congratulations. Maya looked pleased, her slides already queued up on her laptop. David gave a thumbs-up.

Alex sat frozen. There was no mention of the email. No

acknowledgment of the abstract. No rejection, no feedback, just a total, consuming silence. It was as if Alex's ambition hadn't even registered as a blip on Voss's radar.

After the meeting, as the group filed out in a cloud of chatter, Alex lingered. The knot in Alex's stomach was tight, but the need for clarity was stronger.

"Dr. Voss," Alex asked, keeping the tone light. "I sent an abstract earlier this week—did you have a chance to look at it?"

Voss looked up from his laptop. His expression was neutral, his eyes flicking briefly to the open door as if gauging whether there were witnesses.

"Yes, I saw it," Voss said. His voice was calm, devoid of the camaraderie from their first meeting. "It was solid work, Alex. But the symposium committee looks for established results. Maya's piece is simply further along. We have to be strategic about who we put forward."

He smiled thinly, a flash of teeth without warmth. "Keep building. You're doing good support work. Maybe next time."

Alex nodded, throat tight, the words tasting like ash. *Support work.* The demotion was subtle but absolute.

That evening, back in the cramped apartment with the hum of traffic outside, Alex scrolled through the department calendar on their phone. The symposium had been announced two weeks earlier. The deadline for internal review had been five days ago.

Alex realized with a jolt that Maya and David hadn't just whipped up their presentations overnight. They had known. The inner circle had known the exact deadline, the preferred format, and the committee's leanings weeks in advance. Information had flowed to them in whispers, in private Slack channels, in closed-door meetings. Alex had been left to guess, and by the time Alex guessed, the door was already locked.

The fracture wasn't dramatic. There was no shouting, no accusation of incompetence. It was just a small door quietly closed, a small light turned away. But something had shifted irreversibly. The hallway, once wide open with possibility, had begun to narrow.

2. Analysis — The Yellow Light Phase

The first fractures of Stacking are rarely loud or visible. They do not arrive as confrontations, formal rejections, or documented misconduct. If Voss had screamed at Alex, Alex would have had a story to tell HR. Instead, Voss simply withheld information.

These fractures arrive as absences, delays, silences, and gentle deflections. They are small enough to rationalize ("He's just busy") but cumulative enough to erode the target's standing. This phase is known as the **Yellow Light Phase**. The system is not yet stopping you; it is tapping the brakes, testing to see if you will accept a slower velocity.

The primary mechanism at work here is **Information Asymmetry**.

In a healthy institution, information is a public utility. Deadlines, opportunities, and criteria are broadcast to all. In a Stacked institution, information is a private asset. The gatekeeper controls the flow of knowledge like a valve. He opens it wide for the "Loyalty Class" (Maya and David), ensuring they are always prepared, always early, and always aligned. He closes it for the independent thinker (Alex), ensuring they are always reactive, always late, and always guessing.

This creates a structural disadvantage that looks like a personal failure. When Alex submits the abstract late or incomplete compared to Maya's polished presentation, it confirms the narrative that Alex is "not quite ready." The sabotage is hidden behind the appearance of merit.

This phase also triggers a profound psychological state known as **Cognitive Dissonance**.

Alex is torn between two conflicting realities. Reality A is the "Architect Speech," where Voss told Alex they were brilliant and chosen. Reality B is the symposium exclusion, where Voss treated Alex as a nuisance. The human mind hates this contradiction. To resolve the tension, the victim often turns the blame inward. Alex thinks: *Maybe I really am just doing support work. Maybe I'm not as good as I thought. If I work harder, I can get back to Reality A.*

This self-blame is the fuel of the stacking machine. It keeps the victim working harder for a reward that has already been withdrawn.

Furthermore, this dynamic relies on **Pluralistic Ignorance**. In the meeting, everyone likely saw that Alex was excluded. But because no one spoke up, and everyone applauded Maya, the group created a false consensus that the decision was fair. The silence of the bystanders reinforced the validity of the exclusion. Alex felt alone not because the room was empty, but because the room was complicit.

3. Empowerment Insight — From Reaction to Observation

The natural human reaction to the "Yellow Light" is to speed up—to work harder, apologize more, and beg for inclusion. This is exactly what the system expects. It relies on your anxiety to force you into compliance.

The empowerment comes when you shift from **Reaction** to **Observation**.

There is a moment—quiet, private, undeniable—when the newcomer realizes the welcome was conditional. The hallway feels wider. The fluorescent hum louder. The first fracture is no longer hypothetical; it is experienced.

This moment is not defeat. It is clarity. It marks the shift from participant to observer—from someone trying to fit in to someone beginning to see the architecture for what it is.

When you feel the hallway narrow, do not run faster. Stop and look at the walls.

- **Document the Silence:** Note the date you sent the email and the date you received the non-reply.
- **Trace the Information:** Notice who knew about the deadline and how.
- **Reject the Blame:** Understand that your "lateness" was manufactured by the information blockade.

The labyrinth is patient. It narrows slowly, hoping you won't notice until you are pinned. But the moment you name the narrowing; you stop being lost inside it. You begin to map it. And a map is the first step toward an exit.

8

Chapter 8

THE NETWORK REVEALS ITSELF

Loyalty as Performance

1. **The Vignette — The Closing of the Blinds**

Months had passed since the symposium exclusion, and the lab had settled into a new, colder geometry. Alex had found a rhythm of survival: head down, data in, questions rare and carefully worded. The lab felt smaller now, the spaces between benches seemingly widened by silence. There were fewer casual conversations, more solitary hours spent in the hum of equipment, and the occasional clink of glassware became the only soundtrack to long stretches of isolation.

One Friday afternoon, with the air thick with the chemical tang of buffers and the low buzz of the incubator, Alex walked past the glass-walled conference room on the way to the cold room, arms full of ice buckets and sample tubes.

Through the half-open blinds, a tableau was set. The inner circle was gathered around Voss: Maya, two senior postdocs, and a visiting collaborator from a neighboring institution. Laptops were open, papers spread across the table like a feast, and laughter spilled out in short, confident bursts. The room glowed with the warm light of shared purpose—heads close together, fingers pointing at screens, nods of agreement rippling through the group like waves through water.

Alex slowed, pretending to adjust the strap of the ice bucket, heart thudding with a mix of curiosity and dread. The door was ajar just enough to catch fragments of the conversation.

"...priority access to the new sequencer next quarter... recommendation letter draft ready for the Nature submission... we need to lock in the panel slot before the deadline."

Voss leaned back in his chair, arms crossed, smiling that rare, satisfied smile Alex had come to recognize as the highest form of approval—private, possessive, the look of a gardener surveying a well-tended plot. The group nodded in perfect sync, one postdoc already typing notes, another pulling up a shared calendar. The conversation flowed effortlessly, a seamless choreography of deference and mutual reinforcement.

Then, Voss glanced toward the door.

His eyes narrowed for a split second, locking onto Alex for the briefest instant. The moment stretched, long enough for Alex to feel exposed, seen, and judged. Without a word, Voss reached over and adjusted the blinds. He didn't slam them. He didn't look angry. He simply tilted the wand gently, almost casually, until the slats rotated shut.

The gap closed. The message was delivered: *This space is not yours.*

The laughter resumed inside, muffled now, a private world sealed off.

Later that evening, Alex sat alone in the empty break room, the fluorescent light buzzing overhead like an insect trapped in glass. On the laptop screen, the department's shared drive was open. A folder labeled "Internal Opportunities" was visible to everyone in the directory. But when Alex clicked it, a gray dialogue box appeared: *Access Denied. You do not have permission to view this folder.*

A quick search of the lab's private Slack channel—the one Alex had been added to months ago but rarely used—revealed the mechanics of the exclusion. A pinned message from three weeks earlier read: *Symposium abstract deadline this Friday—let me know if you want feedback before submission.*

Alex had never seen it. The channel was flooded with hundreds of messages about lunch orders and memes. The crucial announcement was buried, visible only if you knew to look, or if someone had tagged you. Information had not been withheld; it had been camouflaged.

The next week, Maya presented at the symposium. The talk was solid, though Alex noticed their own protocol tweak was buried in the methods section, unacknowledged—a footnote in someone else's story. Afterward, the group went out for celebratory drinks at the campus bar, the same place Alex had once imagined joining them.

Walking past the window on the way home, Alex saw them through the glass. Voss sat at the head of the table, raising a glass. The circle laughed, phones out, capturing the moment for social media. The image was lit by warm amber light, a perfect portrait of academic camaraderie.

Alex kept walking, the cold night air sharp against their skin, a hollow ache spreading in their chest. But beneath the pain, there was a new realization. The network had finally revealed itself—not through confrontation, but through an exclusion so practiced it felt like gravity. The inner circle wasn't just a group of friends. It was a system. It was a performance.

It was a closed loop that fed itself, sustained itself, and protected itself. And Alex was outside it, watching the light from a distance, the warmth never meant to reach them.

2. Analysis — The Choreography of Control

The network does not reveal itself all at once. It appears in fragments, in the corner of the eye: a door gently pushed shut, a conversation that stops when you enter, an opportunity shared in whispers. This chapter marks the moment when the independent thinker moves from sensing fractures to seeing the full architecture of the **Loyalty Class**.

The group Alex witnessed in that conference room is not a casual collection of students. It is a carefully choreographed performance unit. The "Inner Circle" functions less like a research team and more like a royal court, where membership is maintained through constant, visible displays of alignment.

Key to this dynamic is **Loyalty as Performance**. Notice the synchronized behavior Alex observed—the nodding in unison, the shared laughter, the seamless agreement. This is not accidental. In high-control groups, distinct individuality is viewed as a threat to cohesion. Members of the inner circle instinctively learn to mirror the leader's affect and opinions. They finish sentences. They laugh at jokes that aren't funny. This creates an illusion of consensus and intellectual harmony, signaling to outsiders that the group is a monolithic entity. If you disagree with the leader, you are not just disagreeing with one person; you are disagreeing with the "team."

This performance is sustained by the **Language of the Network**. The inner circle develops a shared shorthand—inside jokes, specific acronyms, and repeated praise of the leader's "vision." Newcomers like Alex are excluded not just because they lack technical knowledge, but because they do not speak the dialect of the group. Every exchange reinforces belonging for the insiders and alienation for the outsiders.

When the network senses a potential intruder—an independent thinker, a skeptic, or simply someone who has not sworn fealty—it activates its **Defensive Reflexes**. These are the network's immune response. We saw this when Voss closed the blinds. It was a low-effort, high-impact signal. Other reflexes include the "conversation pause" when an outsider approaches, or the "email cooling," where responses become shorter and more formal. These actions are rarely coordinated in a conspiratorial sense; they are emergent. The network protects itself the way an immune system protects the body—quietly, efficiently, and without overt violence.

Structurally, the network relies on **Information Asymmetry** as a source of power. The "Internal Opportunities" folder and the buried Slack message highlight how the stacker controls the flow of knowledge. Deadlines, funding calls, and reviewer feedback are shared informally with loyalists first. Public announcements are delayed or incomplete for outsiders. This ensures that loyalists are always one step ahead, appearing more competent and prepared, while independents are left playing catch-up. This asymmetry is engineered to reward loyalty and punish independence, making the stacker the conductor of everyone's career tempo.

3. Empowerment Insight — From Naivety to Mapping

The revelation of the network is often the most painful stage of the journey. It brings a mix of confusion, anger, and profound loneliness. The realization that *"I am seen, but not wanted"* is an existential blow to anyone who entered academia seeking community.

However, this clarity is also the turning point. The network is no longer a mystery; it is a hierarchy. It rewards obedience and punishes independence. It sees the thinker not as a colleague, but as a variable that does not fit the equation.

Once you see the network as a performance, it loses much of its power. You can stop seeking entry into a system that was designed to exclude you. You can stop blaming yourself for "missing" the Slack message and realize you were never meant to see it.

The empowerment comes when you switch from trying to **join** the network to **mapping** it.

- **Observe the performance:** Watch who nods when the leader speaks. Watch who laughs first.
- **Track the information flow:** Note who gets the "soft" deadlines and who gets the hard ones.
- **Respect the closed door:** Do not try to pry open the blinds. Instead, realize that what is happening behind them is not magic; it is merely the maintenance of control.

The moment you see the network clearly is the moment you stop trying to belong inside it. You realize that the warmth behind the glass is artificial, and the cold air outside, while sharp, is at least real. You stop trying to audition for a play you do not want to be in, and you start building your own stage.

9

Chapter 9

THE BREAKING ATTEMPT

Escalation, Sabotage, and the Trojan Horse

1. The Vignette — The Quiet Siege

The lab had transformed from a workplace into a site of quiet siege. Alex still arrived early, still ran the assays with mechanical precision, and still documented every step in color-coded notebooks. But the atmosphere had thickened. The air felt heavier, the fluorescent lights colder, and the physical space between benches seemed to have widened.

Dr. Voss no longer called on Alex in meetings. Emails went unanswered for weeks. When Alex finally submitted a draft for the group manuscript, it came back three weeks later, unrecognizable—stripped of Alex's voice and rewritten in Voss's terse authority.

One morning, Alex opened the shared drive to find a new

task list pinned at the top: routine calibrations, data cleaning, inventory checks. It was work that would consume weeks, offering no authorship and no visibility. "It's just support stuff," Maya had whispered, her eyes flicking toward Voss's closed door. "Voss said we need it done."

Desperate for a lifeline, Alex decided to look for a way out. A prestigious fellowship at a national institute had just opened up. It was the perfect escape hatch. But it required a recommendation letter from the current supervisor.

Alex stood outside Voss's office, heart pounding, rehearsing the request. When Alex entered and asked for the letter, Voss didn't get angry. He didn't refuse. He smiled—that same warm, dangerous smile from the very first day.

"Of course, Alex," Voss said, leaning back. "I'd be happy to support you. You've done... steady work here. Send me the application details. I'll make sure it gets to the right person."

Alex left the office flooded with relief. *He's not sabotaging me,* Alex thought. *He's helping me leave. Maybe I was wrong about everything.*

Two weeks later, the rejection letter from the fellowship arrived. It was a standard form letter, but a friend in the administration later let something slip: "It was weird, Alex. You were on the shortlist. But then there was a phone call."

Alex sat at the bench, holding the rejection email, staring at the "support stuff" list. The realization hit like a physical blow. The recommendation letter hadn't been a favor. It had been a tracking device.

2. Analysis — The Mechanics of the Squeeze

Every institution eventually reaches a moment when it decides whether a person will be absorbed or expelled. For the independent thinker, this is the **Breaking Attempt**. It is the escalation from passive exclusion to active containment.

The primary tool is the **Bureaucratic Squeeze**. Forms are "lost," deadlines are miscommunicated, and requirements change at the last minute. The target spends all their energy navigating the maze rather than doing the work. Simultaneously, the **Reputational Undercurrent** intensifies. Whispers circulate about the target being "difficult" or "unstable," narratives that are impossible to refute because they are never spoken directly.

But the most sophisticated weapon in the Stacker's arsenal—and the one that traps the most victims—is the **Trojan Horse Recommendation**.

The Stacker knows that an open refusal to write a letter looks suspicious. It signals to the world that there is a conflict. Instead, the Stacker agrees to write the letter. They may even show the victim a draft that looks technically positive, praising "hard work" and "technical skills."

This agreement serves a darker purpose: **Intelligence Gathering.**

By agreeing to write the letter, the Stacker forces the victim to reveal their escape route. *Where are you applying? Who is the hiring manager? Which lab is this for?*

Once the Stacker has the coordinates, the Shadow Network activates.

The written letter gets the victim the interview.

But the *phone call* destroys the offer.

The Stacker calls their contact at the company or the other university—often a member of the "Alumni Cartel" discussed in Chapter 5—and delivers the real message off the record:

"Alex is talented, but... unstable. A trouble-maker. Not one of us."

Because the Stacker has a reputation for "brilliance" and bringing in grants, their word is treated as law.

The job offer evaporates. The victim is left confused, holding a copy of the "good" letter, never realizing that the letter was simply the bait used to locate them so the sniper could take the shot.

But the sabotage doesn't always come as a destroyed offer.

Sometimes the network chooses a more elegant cruelty: instead of blocking the opportunity, they green-light it – but in a way designed to fail.

They prompt the company to extend an offer that seems promising at first glance, but underneath the surface it is structurally empty, crafted to extract the victim's knowledge without providing a viable future. The offer that looks promising on paper but is structurally hollow: unstable funding, impossible deliverables, or a temporary role with no path forward. The victim accepts, grateful and hopeful, unaware that the collapse has already been scripted.

Months later, the layoff arrives, or the contract "cannot be renewed," or the performance review is quietly poisoned by the same whisper that opened the door.

The victim is pushed out, and the Shadow Network collects the outcome it engineered:

"See? He can't stay in one place."

This allows the Stacker to maintain the façade of the benevolent mentor while actively destroying the victim's future.

It keeps the victim trapped in the lab, dependent on the Stacker, wondering why they can not seem to get a break, never realizing their application package is wiretapped, their trajectory monitored, and every exit pre-collapsed in advance.

The Breaking Attempt does not just try to crush the spirit; it tries to seal the exits. And it uses the victim's own hope as the lock.

10

Chapter 10

UNDERSTANDING THE GAME

Clarity as the Turning Point

1. The Vignette — The Ghost in the Machine

The breaking attempt had stretched into weeks that felt like months, blurring the line between days. Alex moved through the lab like a ghost in their own life—arriving early to avoid the awkward silence of the hallway, working late to avoid the coordinated departures of the inner circle, and speaking only when absolutely necessary. The task list of "support stuff" had grown into a daily grind of calibrations, inventory logs, and data cleaning—work that required immense precision but offered no ownership, no story, and no future. Each completed item felt like a small surrender, another brick laid in a wall Alex hadn't chosen to build.

One night, the lab was empty. The only sounds were the low,

rhythmic hum of the -80°C freezer and the distant clatter of a ventilation fan that sounded like a mechanical heartbeat. Alex sat at the bench, bathed in the blue glow of the monitor, staring at the latest manuscript draft.

The title page was a hierarchy made visible: Voss and Maya's names at the top in bold; Alex's name buried deep in the acknowledgments, reduced to the phrase "technical assistance." The cursor blinked over a sentence in the discussion section—a sentence Alex had written months earlier in a fever of inspiration. It had been rewritten in Voss's voice. The idea remained, but the authorship had been scrubbed clean.

Alex highlighted the sentence, staring at it until the words blurred. The impulse to delete it, to fight for it, to send an angry email surged—and then, just as quickly, receded. It was replaced by a strange, sudden stillness.

Alex deleted the highlight. They didn't close the file in defeat. Instead, they minimized it and opened a blank document.

For the first time, Alex began typing—not for the lab, not for Voss, not for the grant committee—but for themselves. *October 12: Symposium Abstract ignored. November 3: Protocol B credit reassigned to Maya. November 10: Authorship meeting—'Gift' narrative used. December 1: Support task list assigned without discussion.*

Line by line, the chaos began to organize itself. Dates. Emails. Missed opportunities. Silences. The pattern emerged from the white space, stark and undeniable. This wasn't a series of unfortunate events. It wasn't bad luck. It wasn't a personality clash.

It was a system.

It was a machine designed to harvest labor from the independent and funnel credit to the compliant. Every delay, every tone shift, every "lost" email had a function. The confusion Alex had felt for months wasn't a personal failing; it was the intended output of the machine. The gaslighting was the smoke; the isolation was the wall; the bureaucracy was the lock.

Alex leaned back, the chair creaking in the empty room. The exhaustion was still there, heavy in the bones. The anger still burned low in the chest. But beneath it, something new had taken root: clarity.

The system was not chaotic. It was engineered. And if it was engineered, it was predictable. If it was predictable, it could be navigated.

Alex saved the document, titling it simply "Observations." They closed the laptop and stood up. The lab looked different now. The high ceilings, the expensive equipment, the framed awards on the wall—they no longer felt imposing. They felt like props on a stage. The labyrinth had not changed, but Alex had.

Alex walked out into the corridor, the fluorescent hum still buzzing, but it no longer felt oppressive. It felt ordinary. The machine had been seen. And once seen, it could never again be feared in quite the same way.

2. Analysis — Decoding the Architecture

The breaking attempt does not break the independent thinker. It reveals the rules. For the first time, the pressure is not just endured; it is understood. The confusion that characterizes the earlier stages of Stacking transforms into a cold, forensic clarity. The system ceases to be a storm of random, hurtful events and reveals itself as a structured game with discernible moves, incentives, and weaknesses.

This chapter marks the essential pivot: the shift from being shaped by the system to decoding it, from emotional entanglement to strategic detachment.

The turning point begins with a fundamental internal realization: **"It's Not Me — It's the System."**

For months, the target asks the wrong questions: *What did I do wrong? Why don't they like me? How can I fix this?* These questions assume the problem is personal. The turning point arrives when the questions shift: *What purpose does this behavior serve? Who benefits from this dynamic? What pattern am I part of?*

When Alex types out the timeline, the self-blame dissolves. The problem is structural. The behavior of the Stacker is not a judgment on Alex's worth; it is a mechanism of resource extraction.

With this shift, the independent thinker begins to see the **Architecture Behind the Behavior**. The characters in the drama shed their masks. The Gatekeeper (Voss) is no longer a mentor failing at his job; he is a manager of loyalty and legacy, driven by a metabolic need for admiration and control. The Inner Circle is not a group of "mean colleagues"; they are enforcers of hierarchy, policing boundaries to protect their own precarious status. The Bureaucracy is not a neutral administrative hurdle; it is a weaponized tool of delay and containment.

The thinker also begins to recognize the specific **Psychological Tools** at play.

- **Gaslighting** is identified not as a misunderstanding, but as a deliberate distortion of reality designed to induce cognitive dissonance.
- **Triangulation** is seen as a tactical move to pit students against one another, preventing unity.
- **Scarcity Manipulation** reveals itself as a behavioral economics trick—creating an artificial shortage of opportunity

to increase compliance.

- **Fear Conditioning** is exposed as a training method, using subtle punishments to shape obedience.

These are not random cruelties. They are techniques. They are predictable, repeatable, and effective on most people. But they lose their efficacy on those who understand them.

This understanding exposes the system's greatest weakness: **Its power depends on invisibility.** Stacking thrives in the shadows of ambiguity. It relies on the victim staying silent, confused, and isolated. Once the victim sees the mechanism, the spell breaks. The system is revealed to be fragile, held together only by perception and silence.

This leads to the **Internal Shift: From Reaction to Detachment**. The thinker undergoes a transformation the system cannot anticipate. They stop seeking approval, because they realize approval is a currency they cannot afford. They stop explaining themselves, because they realize the system is committed to misunderstanding them. They stop trying to belong to a network that was never designed to include them.

Instead, they adopt a posture of **Strategic Detachment**. This is not coldness; it is clarity. It allows the thinker to observe manipulation without absorbing it. When the Stacker offers a backhanded compliment, the thinker records it as data rather than feeling it as an insult. When the inner circle excludes them, the thinker notes the tactic rather than internalizing the rejection.

As the thinker becomes more aware, the power dynamics shift. Gaslighting fails because the thinker trusts their own perception. Triangulation fails because the thinker refuses to compete. Isolation fails because the thinker begins to look outward, building alliances beyond the institution's walls.

The system begins to sense this shift. It cannot break what it cannot control. Fear was its only real weapon. Without fear, the machine grinds to a halt.

3. Empowerment Insight: Clarity Is Stronger Than Conformity

This moment is the beginning of true sovereignty. The breaking attempt does not end the story; it begins the real one. The independent thinker reclaims their agency not by fighting the system on its own terms, but by understanding it so thoroughly that its traps become visible.

The moment you stop asking "Why is this happening to me?" and start asking "How does this machine work?" is the moment the machine loses its hold. The game is rigged. But once you see the rigging, you stop playing by their rules. You start writing your own.

11

Chapter 11

BECOMING UNSTACKABLE

The Decentralized Self

1. The Vignette — The Orbit Shift

The shift was not dramatic. There was no single day when Alex stormed out of the lab, no explosive confrontation with Voss, no tearful resignation letter left on a desk. To the casual observer, Alex looked exactly the same: sitting at the same bench, pipetting the same clear liquids, staring at the same screens.

But the internal geometry had changed.

Alex began arriving at 9:30 AM instead of 8:00 AM—not to avoid work, but to avoid the ritual of early deference, the unspoken requirement to be seen waiting for Voss to arrive. The first hour of the day was no longer spent checking the lab Slack channel in a panic of FOMO (Fear Of Missing Out).

Instead, Alex spent that hour at a coffee shop three blocks away, working on a private laptop. On the screen was a document titled "External Pathways." It was a list of conferences Voss never attended, open calls for collaboration in adjacent fields, and online communities of open-science advocates.

When Alex did arrive at the lab, the work was efficient, precise, and detached. When Voss assigned another round of "support stuff"—inventorying the chemical cabinet—Alex completed it without the previous over-investment. There were no extra color-coded labels, no "above and beyond" formatting. The task was done to standard, and not a millimeter more. Alex realized that perfectionism in a toxic system is not a virtue; it is a tax.

One afternoon, Alex sat in a virtual seminar hosted by a university in London. It was technically during "lab hours," but Alex had headphones on and a spreadsheet open to look busy. In the chat sidebar, a postdoc named Elena asked a question about the very structural dynamics Alex had been studying.

Alex took a breath and typed a direct message: *"I've been working on a protocol that addresses that exact artifact. Happy to share the code if you're interested."*

The reply came two minutes later: *"That would be amazing. Email me?"*

That night, Alex did something forbidden by the unwritten laws of the Enclave. They uploaded the protocol redesign to a preprint server, *bioRxiv*. First author: Alex Reed. Sole author. It was a methodological piece, small enough that Voss couldn't claim ownership of the data, but significant enough to be useful. The upload timestamp glowed on the screen like a small declaration of independence.

A week later, Voss walked by Alex's bench. "Alex, I didn't see you at the happy hour last night. We missed you."

In the past, this comment would have triggered a spiral of guilt. *I should have gone. I need to show face. I'm losing my standing.*

Now, Alex simply looked up from the microscope, expression calm. "I had a prior commitment. How was it?"

Voss blinked, expecting an apology and finding only politeness. "It was... fine. Good team bonding." He lingered for a moment, sensing the change but unable to name it. The hook—the emotional tug that usually reeled Alex back in—had snagged on nothing. Voss walked away, unsettled.

Alex returned to the microscope. The "prior commitment" had been a Zoom call with Elena in London, sketching out a potential review paper.

The lab still existed. Voss still presided like a king. The inner circle still performed their loyalty dance. But Alex no longer lived inside their gravitational pull. They had begun to orbit something else: their own center.

The transformation was invisible to the room, but Alex felt it: a loosening in the chest, a quietening of the constant internal questioning, a growing sense of sovereignty. The system had tried to break them. Instead, it had decentralized them.

2. Analysis — The Strategy of Decentralization

There comes a moment when the independent thinker realizes the system cannot be changed from within—not by compliance, not by confrontation, and often not even by formal grievance. The institution is designed to protect itself. The only path to freedom is to outgrow the container.

This is the state of **Becoming Unstackable**.

To be Unstackable does not mean you are invincible. It means you are **Decentralized**.

A "Stacked" individual is a centralized node. Their entire professional existence—funding, reputation, visa status, future job prospects, emotional validation—flows through a single gatekeeper (the Stacker). If the Stacker cuts the line, the individual is deleted.

An "Unstackable" individual is a distributed network. Their reputation lives in external communities; their validation comes from independent work; their opportunities flow from multiple sources. If the Stacker cuts the line, they lose a connection, not their existence.

This transformation requires a shift from **Survival Mode** to **Strategic Operation**, governed by specific protocols.

a. The "Ghost Ship" Strategy (Parallel Pathways). The stacker's power comes from your lack of alternatives. To break this, you must build a project that owes nothing to the lab.

- **The Action:** Alex writing the preprint and contacting Elena is the "Ghost Ship" strategy. It is a vessel built in secret, using your own resources (time, intellect), launched from a port the Stacker does not control.
- **The Impact:** When you have an external collaboration, you no longer *need* the Stacker's project to succeed. This indifference makes you impossible to manipulate.

b. Strategic Invisibility (The "Gray Rock" Method). Visibility is not always power. In a hostile environment, visibility is vulnerability.

- **The Action:** When Voss fished for guilt ("We missed you"), Alex offered no emotion, no excuse, and no information. This is "Gray Rocking"—becoming as uninteresting and unreactive as a rock.

- **The Impact:** Narcissists feed on reaction (supply). If you stop reacting, they stop targeting you because you are a "low-nutrient" source of supply.

c. The 20% Rule (Building External Networks). A node connected to only one hub is easily isolated.

- **The Action:** Alex dedicated time to the virtual seminar in London. The rule is simple: **Dedicate 20% of your energy to non-institutional activities.**
- **The Impact:** External networks provide reality checks. When Alex talks to Elena, Elena confirms that Alex's ideas are valuable. This counteracts the gaslighting inside the lab.

d. Excellence as a Shield. The most common mistake victims make is to stop working or to produce poor work out of spite. This is a trap. It gives the Stacker ammunition to fire you for "incompetence."

- **The Action:** Alex completed the inventory task "to standard."
- **The Impact:** High-quality work protects you. It makes you harder to dismiss. But crucially, Alex stopped doing *extra* work. Excellence is the shield; boundaries are the sword.

e. Emotional Immunity The final shift is internal. The thinker develops a new kind of strength—not hardness, but discernment.

- **The Action:** Alex stopped scanning the room for Voss's

approval.

- **The Impact:** When you realize that the Stacker's behavior is a reflection of *their* pathology, not *your* worth, you become immune to their tone. You stop internalizing the silence.

f. Rewriting the Narrative The system tries to label the independent thinker as "difficult" or "not a team player." The Unstackable thinker reclaims these labels.

- "Difficult" becomes **Discerning**.
- "Not aligned" becomes **Self-Directed**.
- "Unpredictable" becomes **Strategic**.

3. Empowerment Insight: Freedom is Internal

This chapter teaches that freedom is not a grant from an institution. It is an internal architecture. The system can narrow the hallway, but it cannot shrink your orbit once you stop needing its gravity.

Alex did not defeat Voss in a battle. Alex simply rendered Voss irrelevant. The Stacker continued to play his game, but he was playing it alone. Alex had moved to a different board.

You are no longer a variable in someone else's equation. You are the architect of your own.

12

Chapter 12

RECLAIMING POWER

Sovereignty Restored

1. The Vignette — The Silence of the Warning Light

The change was quiet, almost invisible at first—even to Alex. They still came to the lab, still ran experiments under the humming vents, and still met deadlines with professional rigor. But the internal frequency had shifted. The knot of anxiety that used to tighten in the solar plexus every time Dr. Voss walked past no longer formed. The reflexive urge to explain, to justify every small decision, to scan the room for approval before speaking had faded like a fever breaking in the night.

One morning, the test came. Alex arrived to find another "support" task list waiting in the inbox—more calibrations, more manual logging, more invisible labor designed to consume time without generating credit. In the past, Alex would have stayed late to finish it, resentful but compliant, hoping that obedience would eventually buy freedom.

This time, Alex simply read the email, took a sip of coffee, and hit reply.

Alex cc'd the entire lab group—a move that ensured visibility—and typed a response that was terrifying in its neutrality: *"Completed the previous batch ahead of schedule. Happy to take on more if needed later, but I'm prioritizing finishing my independent analysis this week to meet the preprint deadline. Let me know if there's a deadline conflict."*

There was no apology. No deferential padding. No "I hope that's okay." Just facts, boundaries, and a clear signal of priority.

Alex hit send and waited for the explosion. But the explosion never came. Voss's reply arrived within the hour, shorter than usual: *"Understood. Focus on your analysis."*

There was no follow-up. No redirection. No subtle reprimand in the hallway. The silence felt different this time—not punitive, but empty. It was the silence of a bluff being called. The system had pushed, and for the first time, Alex had not pushed back; Alex had simply stepped aside.

That same week, the *bioRxiv* preprint went live. The title was bold, the data was clean, and the author list was short: **Alex Reed**. The protocol redesign—once absorbed, reframed, and minimized by the lab's hierarchy—was now public, timestamped, and citable.

Within days, the external world responded. Two emails arrived from researchers at other institutions: one requesting the code, another proposing a potential collaboration. Neither message mentioned Voss. Neither message asked for permission. To these strangers, Alex was not a graduate student to be managed, but a peer to be engaged.

Alex printed the acceptance email and pinned it above the bench—not for display, but for a reminder. The paper was modest, but it was *theirs*. Untouched by red ink. Unmediated by loyalty tests. The act of claiming it felt like filling lungs with fresh air after holding one's breath for months.

At the next lab meeting, the dynamic had visibly altered. When Alex spoke about a minor methodological point, the voice was steady, factual, and indifferent to validation. Voss nodded once and moved on. There was no redirection. No chill in the room. The inner circle glanced at each other, uncertain how to treat someone who no longer played the game.

The performance of the loyalty court continued, but Alex was no longer in the audience.

That night, walking home under a clear winter sky, Alex felt the cold air sharp against their face and realized that for the first time in years, they did not feel small. The labyrinth had not disappeared. The walls were still there. But Alex had stopped living inside its gravity. They had begun to reclaim power—not by fighting the system, but by outgrowing it.

2. Analysis — The Anatomy of Reclamation

Power in academia is often misunderstood. People assume it comes from titles, committees, publications, or proximity to famous gatekeepers. We are taught that power is something given to us when we are finally deemed "ready."

But real power—the kind that cannot be taken away—comes from clarity, independence, and the ability to build a life that does not depend on the approval of fragile hierarchies. This is the essence of becoming **Unstackable**. The independent thinker reclaims what the system tried to traffic away: confidence, direction, voice, and future. This process is not about revenge or rebellion; it is about the quiet, disciplined rebuilding of a sovereign identity.

The first step is **Reclaiming the Narrative**. The system spent months trying to define the thinker with labels designed to control. Difficult. Independent. Not aligned. Not a team player. These labels were never objective truths; they were tools of containment. The thinker now rewrites the dictionary. "Difficult" is reclassified as "Discerning." "Independent" ceases to be an insult and becomes a descriptor of "Self-Directed." "Unpredictable" is recognized as "Strategic". By refusing to accept the system's definitions, the thinker strips the labels of their weight.

Simultaneously, the thinker engages in **Reclaiming Time and Focus**. The "Stacking" machine functions by wasting the target's energy on non-productive labor—decoding gossip, anticipating attacks, and defending against gaslighting. The reclaimed thinker stops paying this tax. They redirect that energy into the only things that truly matter: research, writing, skill-building, and network cultivation. Time is the most valuable resource in the intellectual economy, and reclaiming it from the drama of the lab is an act of liberation.

This leads inevitably to **Reclaiming Identity**. The institution often tries to shrink the individual into a compliant role: the obedient student, the grateful subordinate, the silent collaborator. The thinker remembers who they were before the institution tried to reshape them—curious, creative, and whole. Identity becomes a shield. When the stacker attacks, they are attacking a role, not the person.

Perhaps the most practical shift is **Reclaiming Opportunity**.

The stacked individual waits for permission—to publish, to travel, to speak. The reclaimed individual stops waiting. They apply for independent grants. They publish preprints without gatekeeper approval. They collaborate across institutions and explore careers beyond academia. They realize the world is vastly larger than the department, and far more open than the "Enclave" would have them believe.

Finally, there is the **Reclamation of Voice**. The thinker begins to speak again. Not loudly, not aggressively, but clearly. They ask the questions others avoid. They express ideas without the tremor of fear. They advocate for themselves and others. This voice is steady because it is grounded in purpose. The thinker reconnects with the reason they entered this field in the first place—curiosity, discovery, and contribution—replacing the system's demand for obedience with their own demand for meaning.

3. Empowerment Insight — Outgrowing the Gatekeeper

This chapter marks the end of the system's influence and the beginning of the thinker's sovereignty. It demonstrates that reclaiming power is not about defeating the gatekeeper in a battle of wills. It is about outgrowing them.

Independence is not a liability; it is the ultimate strength. The future belongs not to those who conform most perfectly, but to those who remain themselves in the face of pressure.

The system can narrow hallways, close doors, and withhold light. But it cannot contain someone who has stopped needing its gravity. You are no longer inside the machine. You are charting the stars.

13

Chapter 13

A FRAMEWORK FOR FUTURE INDEPENDENT THINKERS

The 10 Principles of Unstackability

1. The Vignette — The Handover

It had been six months since Alex Reed stopped living inside the gravity of Dr. Voss's lab. The physical space remained unchanged—the same fluorescent hum, the same whiteboard equations scrawled in red and blue, the same inner circle performing their rituals of loyalty. But Alex no longer belonged to it. They arrived when needed, contributed exactly what was required by the contract of their stipend, and left without lingering. The task lists still arrived, and Alex completed them efficiently, stripping away the emotional over-investment that had once made them exhausting. Voss's tone had shifted, too, settling into a careful neutrality. He was neither warm nor cold, simply disengaged. The system had stopped trying to break Alex because there was nothing left to grip.

One rainy Tuesday afternoon, Alex received an email from a first-year PhD student named Elena. She was in a different department but had heard Alex speak at a recent graduate union mixer. *"I feel like I'm going crazy,"* the email read. *"My advisor says I'm not a team player because I asked to be second author on a paper I wrote. Can we talk?"*

They met at a coffee shop on the edge of campus, far enough away to be anonymous. Elena looked exactly how Alex felt a year ago: tired, anxious, her shoulders hunched as if expecting a blow. She spent twenty minutes pouring out a chaotic story of gaslighting, shifting deadlines, and confusing praise.

"I just don't know what I'm doing wrong," Elena said, staring at her cooling tea. "Maybe I'm just not cut out for this."

Alex reached into their bag and pulled out a stapled document. It wasn't a scientific paper. It was a distillation of everything the last year had taught them—the "Observations" file, now organized into a cohesive strategy.

"You aren't doing anything wrong," Alex said, sliding the document across the table. "You are being Stacked. And you aren't crazy. You're just looking at the chaotic surface of a very organized machine."

Elena opened the document. The first heading read: *Principle 1: See the System Early.*

"This isn't advice," Alex said gently. "It's a map. It tells you where the traps are so you don't have to fall into them to find out they exist. Read it. Use it. And when you're safe, pass it on."

Elena began to read, and for the first time in an hour, her shoulders dropped. The panic in her eyes was replaced by focus. She wasn't looking at a reflection of her own failure anymore.

She was looking at the blueprints of the prison.

Alex sat back, watching the transformation happen in real-time. The labyrinth hadn't vanished. But for Elena, the lights had just turned on.

2. Analysis — The Protocols of Sovereignty

The journey from victim to independent thinker is not just about courage; it is about technique. Institutions do not operate on logic alone; they operate on predictable psychological mechanisms. To survive and thrive, the independent thinker needs more than resilience—they need a framework.

What follows are the ten core principles of the Unstackable mindset. These are not abstract ideals. They are action protocols designed to dismantle the specific mechanisms of stacking, whether you are facing a Prestige Stacker in Boston or an Enclave Builder in London.

Principle 1: See the System Early (The Detection Protocol)

The most dangerous part of stacking is the time before you recognize it. Stacking relies on your naivety, on your belief that the institution is a meritocracy. Detection destroys the element of surprise.

To operationalize this, conduct a **First 30 Days Audit**. When you enter a new environment, ignore the mission statement and map the behavior. Draw a mental map of the silos: who eats lunch together? Who is never invited to the coffee run? Test the information flow by asking a "dummy question" to a superior—something simple like a deadline date—and cross-reference the answer with a peer. If the dates differ, you have detected Information Asymmetry. Identify the "Golden Child," the student who can do no wrong, and study them not to imitate, but to calibrate your understanding of what the system actually rewards. Usually, it is compliance, not merit.

Principle 2: Understand the Psychology (The Detachment Protocol)

Institutions are run by people, and people are driven by needs. The stacker's behavior is driven by their insecurity, not your inadequacy. When you understand this, you can stop internalizing the abuse.

Activate the **Translation Exercise**. When you receive ambiguous or hurtful feedback, translate it instantly in your notes. When they say, "You're not a team player," write down: *You are not feeding my narcissistic supply.* When they say, "You need to wait your turn," write down: *You are moving faster than I can control.* When they say, "We do things differently here," write down: *I need you to submit to the hierarchy.* This simple act of translation prevents the words from landing on your self-esteem. You stop feeling guilty and start analyzing the tactic.

Principle 3: Build External Networks (The Decentralization Protocol)

A node connected to only one hub is easily isolated. A node connected to many hubs is resilient. The most powerful defense against stacking is not confrontation; it is independence.

Follow the **20% Rule**. Dedicate twenty percent of your working hours to non-institutional activities. Send one "Cold Email" per week to a researcher outside your university or country—not asking for a job, but asking a specific, intelligent question about their work. Join the "Shadow College" of open science forums, Discord servers, or international societies where your supervisor has no influence. If you are in an Enclave Lab, your priority is to find a mentor from a different cultural background to pick the lock of the cultural pressure.

Principle 4: Document Patterns (The Evidence Protocol)

Incidents can be denied. Patterns cannot. Gaslighting fails against data.

Keep a **Black Box Log**. This is a timestamped digital record kept off university servers. Use the "Rule of Three": one incident is an accident; two is a coincidence; three is a pattern. Once you have three entries for the same behavior—three missed emails, three backhanded comments, three exclusions— you have actionable intelligence. This log is not necessarily for retaliation or lawsuits; it is for your own sanity. It is the mirror that reveals the system's behavior without distortion.

Principle 5: Protect Your Identity (The Sovereignty Protocol)

"Institutions" try to colonize your self-image, reshaping you into a compliant version of yourself.

Implement the **Sunday Separation**. Establish one day, or at least distinct hours, where you do zero academic work and engage in a hobby where you are competent and respected— music, sports, volunteering. This is not just leisure; it is a structural reminder that "Academic" is your job, not your soul. When the stacker attacks your professional worth, your core identity remains untouched because it is rooted elsewhere.

Principle 6: Master Strategic Invisibility (The Camouflage Protocol)

Visibility is not always power. In a hostile environment, visibility is vulnerability.

Practice the **Gray Rock Performance**. In meetings with a hostile gatekeeper, become uninteresting. Give short, factual answers. Do not share personal news, future dreams, or emotional reactions. Hide the gold: do not discuss your best independent ideas with the stacker until they are mature enough to be published or protected. If you share them too early, they will be stolen or crushed. You protect your flame by keeping it out of their wind.

Principle 7: Choose Battles (The Energy Protocol)

Not every injustice requires a response. Fighting every slight leads to burnout, which is exactly what the "system" wants.

Apply the **Hill Test**. Before reacting to an injustice, ask: "Is this a hill I am willing to die on?" Ignore the snubs, the rude tones, the petty exclusions; these are bait designed to draw you into a fight you cannot win. Fight only the existential threats: authorship theft, visa threats, safety violations. Wisdom is knowing the difference between a distraction and a disaster.

Principle 8: Build Parallel Pathways (The Exit Protocol)

The stacker's power comes from your lack of alternatives.

Adopt the **Ghost Ship Strategy**. Quietly build a project that owes nothing to the lab. Write the independent preprint on weekends. Maintain an active industry profile. Interview once a year even if you don't intend to leave, just to prove to yourself that you are hireable. A person with an exit strategy cannot be held hostage.

Never blindly trust a gatekeeper to write a "good" letter. Before you have them send a recommendation to your dream job, have them send one to a low-stakes "dummy" application or a trusted peer posing as a recruiter.

Have that peer ask for a phone call. Listen to what the Stacker says *off the record*. If the written letter says "solid researcher" but the voice on the phone says "difficult personality," you have detected a Trojan Horse. Do not use that reference again. Burn that bridge before it burns you.

Principle 9: Reframe the Narrative (The Branding Protocol)

The system will try to define you with labels like "difficult" or "unfocused."

Create a **Public Portfolio**. Control your own digital footprint.

Create a personal website or blog. Curate your own narrative. If the stacker says you are "unfocused," your public portfolio shows "interdisciplinary breadth." Ensure that when someone Googles you, your story comes up first, not your advisor's lab page.

Principle 10: Become Unstackable (The Integration Protocol)

To be unstackable is to shift your operating state from permission-seeking to sovereign.

Adopt the **Sovereign Mindset**. Shift your language from asking "Can I do this?" to informing "I am planning to do this." Treat your PhD or your job as a client contract, not a feudal vow. You are a consultant delivering services, not a subject serving a king.

3. Empowerment Insight — The Map is Yours

This chapter is a gift to the reader—a guide for navigating institutions without losing oneself. It teaches that stacking is predictable, manipulation is recognizable, and independence is strength. The protagonist's journey is not unique; it is universal. And this framework ensures that those who follow will walk with eyes open, identity intact, and power reclaimed.

The framework is yours. Use it. Share it. And never again let a single gatekeeper define your orbit.

14

Chapter 14

A VISION FOR REFORM

Rebuilding an Academic System Worthy of Free Thinkers

1. The Vignette — The Coalition of the Willing

It had been nearly a year since Alex Reed walked out of Dr. Voss's orbit for good. The lab still existed in its hermetic seal— the same fluorescent hum, the same whiteboard equations scrawled in red and blue, the same inner circle performing their rituals of loyalty. But Alex no longer belonged to it. They had finished the PhD in a different department, under a new advisor who valued questions over obedience and viewed mentorship as a service, not a transaction.

The dissertation was published open access. First-author papers accumulated. Invitations arrived from institutions Alex had never imagined applying to. But the victory felt incomplete. Survival was not enough; Alex wanted change.

One rainy evening, Alex sat in a small apartment in a new city, laptop open to a draft email. The subject line read: *"Proposal: Transparent Mentorship and Authorship Auditing Pilot."*

The body of the email was simple but precise. It outlined a voluntary program for labs willing to open their doors to sunlight: contribution logs timestamped at the start of projects, authorship agreements signed before data generation began, anonymous feedback channels for mentees, and an external review of publication patterns. It wasn't revolutionary in a technical sense; the tools already existed. It was revolutionary in a political sense because it replaced trust with verification.

Alex attached the "Observations" document—now a polished, twelve-page summary of patterns, mechanisms, and lessons learned from the trenches—and hit send.

The recipients were a small, disparate coalition: early-career researchers Alex had met through open-science forums, two sympathetic associate professors from different universities who had quietly voiced their own frustrations, and a program officer from a private foundation interested in academic integrity.

The reply came the next morning from one of the professors: *"This is overdue. Let's meet. I know people who would fund a pilot."*

Alex leaned back, the screen light reflecting in their eyes. For so long, the system had felt like a monolith—an unmovable object that crushed anyone who pushed against it. But looking at that reply, Alex realized the monolith was cracked. The system had tried to break them. Instead, it had given them clarity. And with clarity came the possibility of redesign.

This wasn't about revenge. It wasn't about exposing Voss or burning down the department. It was about obsolescence. Alex realized that the labyrinth didn't need to be destroyed; it needed to be bypassed. By building a new path—one paved with transparency and lit by accountability—the old, dark hallways would simply become empty.

Alex had stopped living inside the machine and had begun to build the engine that would replace it.

2. Analysis — The Collapse of the Old Deal

Every institution eventually reaches a tipping point where its internal contradictions become impossible to ignore. Academia has arrived at that point.

On paper, the modern university is a beacon of enlightenment. It publicly celebrates curiosity, innovation, diversity of thought, and intellectual courage. It claims to be the one place in society where the pursuit of truth supersedes the pursuit of profit or power. Yet, the internal reality for many scholars is a mirror image of these ideals. The system operates through rigid hierarchies, enforced conformity, political alliances, and silent networks of control.

This contradiction is no longer sustainable. A system cannot thrive on the brilliance of free thinkers while simultaneously empowering structures that suppress them. We are witnessing the collapse of the "Old Deal"—the tacit agreement that junior scholars would endure exploitation in exchange for a guaranteed career. That guarantee is gone, but the exploitation remains.

The root of this failure is a governance model built on hypocrisy. We market "critical thinking" to undergraduates while punishing it in graduate students. We champion "academic freedom" for tenured professors while allowing them to hold the visas of international students hostage. This is not merely a moral failure; it is a structural defect. A system cannot produce truth while punishing those who speak it.

The old model relied on assumptions that no longer hold

water. It assumed that gatekeepers always act in good faith, yet provided no safeguards for when they do not. It assumed that hierarchy ensures quality, when in reality, it often protects mediocrity and punishes originality. It assumed that closed networks are harmless, ignoring how they distort opportunity and create intellectual monocultures. And it assumed that bureaucracy ensures fairness, even as bureaucracy became the primary tool for delay and narrative control.

Reforming this broken architecture is not about punishing bad individuals. It is about redesigning the environment so that "Stacking" becomes impossible. A healthy academic system must be built on three non-negotiable pillars.

a. The First Pillar is Transparency. Sunlight is the only disinfectant that works on Stacking. We need systems where hiring, authorship, and funding decisions are visible. We need publicly accessible contribution logs for all collaborative projects, so that the history of an idea cannot be rewritten by the person with the most power. We need annual audits of opportunity distribution to reveal who is being excluded. When the mechanics of decision-making are hidden, corruption is inevitable. When they are visible, fairness becomes the path of least resistance.

b. The Second Pillar is Accountability. Currently, the cost of abusing power in academia is near zero. The "Star Professor" is protected by their grant revenue, while the whistleblower faces career annihilation. This dynamic must invert. We need clear, enforceable consequences for credit theft and retaliation. We need independent oversight bodies with real authority—not internal committees beholden to the department chair. We need to limit the influence of any single gatekeeper by mandating distributed advising and term limits on mentorship roles. Accountability breaks the networks of control by introducing risk to the abuser.

c. The Third Pillar is Intellectual Pluralism. The "Lobbies of Thinkers"—those powerful factions that dominate panels, control journals, and enforce consensus—must be dismantled. We must actively reward dissent and unconventional ideas. We must protect minority viewpoints and encourage interdisciplinary risks. By reducing dependence on single mentors and diversifying decision-making bodies, we create an ecosystem where an idea succeeds based on its merit, not its lineage.

This vision requires us to re-center the university around the **Free Thinker**. The future of academia depends on the very people it currently marginalizes: the unconventional, the independent, the interdisciplinary, and the culturally diverse. These are the individuals who create new fields and disrupt stagnation. A reformed system must protect them through multiple mentorship pathways, independent funding channels, and robust protections against retaliation.

We must also reimagine academic leadership. The role of a professor must shift from gatekeeper to steward, from controller to facilitator. Leaders should be selected not for their ability to accumulate power, but for their ability to nurture it in others. Trust cannot be restored through slogans or glossy brochures. It must be rebuilt through architecture—through independent ombuds offices, external audits, and anonymous reporting systems that actually work.

This is not a utopian fantasy. It is a necessity. The world is changing faster than the university. We face global crises—food security, pandemics, artificial intelligence inequality—that demand bold, unconstrained inquiry. If universities do not reform, they will become irrelevant, bypassed by new models of discovery that value speed and truth over hierarchy and tradition.

The vision for the future university is simple: it is a place where dissent is valued, originality is rewarded, and networks cannot control opportunity. It is a place where the free thinker is the center, not the margin.

Reform is not about fixing a broken system; it is about building a new one that renders the old one obsolete. Hypocrisy ends when we demand better—not with rage, but with vision. The system can be rebuilt. It begins with those who refuse to be broken.

15

Chapter 15

THE NEW COMMAND

AI in the Governance of the Future University

1. The Vignette — The Dashboard of Truth

The email arrived on a quiet Tuesday morning, dropping into Alex's inbox with the unassuming ping of a routine notification. The subject line, however, carried the weight of a revolution: *"Pilot Proposal: Transparent Mentorship & Authorship Auditing."*

It came from the small coalition Alex had helped assemble months earlier—a group that had grown from a few frustrated researchers into a disciplined network of twelve scientists across six institutions, backed by a program officer from a private foundation dedicated to academic integrity.

Alex opened the attachment. It was a grant application for $250,000 to fund a two-year pilot program. The core idea was simple but radical: an opt-in platform where laboratories would upload anonymized metadata—project timelines, contribution statements, email response logs, and publication records—into a secure, open-source system.

The AI, trained on models with strict privacy controls, would not read the content of the emails or judge the science. Instead, it would look for patterns. It would flag the structural imbalances that human committees were too polite or too frightened to name. It would detect when a junior researcher contributed seventy percent of the code but received sixth authorship. It would notice when a specific demographic of student was systematically excluded from high-visibility email chains. It would map the silence.

The proposal described a dashboard that would display these patterns not as accusations, but as data points. No names, no public shaming—just clear, undeniable metrics showing where the credit was flowing and where the labor was hiding.

One line in the executive summary stood out to Alex: *"The goal is not punishment, but sunlight. Transparency is the antidote to opacity."*

Alex read the draft twice, feeling a strange mix of pride and disbelief. A year ago, they had been huddled in a cold apartment, documenting these patterns in a private file just to prove to themselves they weren't crazy. Now, those private observations were becoming the architecture of a system-wide intervention. The specific pain of the labyrinth was being transmuted into a map for everyone else.

The email ended with a request: *"We'd like you to lead the data-privacy and ethics section. Your 'Observations' document is already the clearest framework we have."*

Alex stared at the screen, the cursor blinking over the reply button. The lab, Voss, the inner circle—they still existed somewhere, playing their game of loyalty and leverage. But they no longer defined the horizon. Alex had stopped being a variable in someone else's equation.

Now, quietly and deliberately, they were helping rewrite the rules of the game itself. Alex typed two words: *"I'm in."*

2. Analysis — The Algorithm of Accountability

Every era of academia has been defined by a dominant force of governance. The medieval university was ruled by the clergy, ensuring theological alignment. The industrial university was ruled by bureaucracy, ensuring efficiency. The modern university is ruled by networks and gatekeepers, ensuring the reproduction of prestige.

We are now standing on the precipice of the next era. It will be ruled by data—and the intelligence that interprets it.

Artificial Intelligence is often discussed as a tool for research or a threat to student essays. But its most profound application lies in governance. AI represents a new command structure, a layer of oversight capable of piercing the opacity that has protected stackers for decades. It is a machine that can see the invisible walls.

And that is precisely why so many powerful gatekeepers fear it.

For generations, academic power has depended on the ability to hide. Decisions about hiring, funding, and authorship are made in closed rooms, protected by the veil of "professional judgment." This subjectivity is the soil in which Stacking grows. It allows a professor to claim that a favored student is "brilliant" and an independent thinker is "difficult" without ever having to show the evidence. Favoritism leaves no paper trail—until now.

AI disrupts the old order because it makes patterns visible. Bias, exclusion, and credit theft are no longer abstract feelings; they become measurable vectors. An algorithm does not care about a professor's tenure status or their h-index. It simply logs the discrepancy between labor and credit. It makes decisions auditable. When a committee claims they selected a candidate based on merit, the AI can analyze the criteria against the outcome. When a grant is awarded, the system can trace the network connections between the reviewers and the recipient.

This shift transforms the university from a trust-based system to a verification-based system.

The promise of AI governance lies in its potential to democratize opportunity. Imagine a system where evaluation is transparent. Algorithms could track publication quality, contribution levels, teaching effectiveness, and mentorship outcomes—not to replace human judgment, but to anchor it in evidence. Instead of a letter of recommendation, which is often a tool of patronage, a student could present a "Contribution Portfolio" verified by blockchain, showing every line of code, every dataset, and every draft they produced.

This technology also allows for the equitable distribution of opportunity. AI can ensure that funding calls reach every eligible researcher, not just those in the inner circle. It can monitor workload distribution, flagging when a specific student is overburdened with "support tasks" while another is given nothing but high-visibility projects.

Perhaps most critically, AI serves as an early warning system for abuse. Pattern recognition can identify the signatures of toxicity long before a formal complaint is filed. It can detect the statistical anomalies of a lab where international students stay twice as long as domestic ones, or where women are consistently under-credited on patents. It can spot the silence—the sudden drop in email activity or the removal of a student from calendar invites—that signals a social freeze-out.

However, we must be clear about the mechanics. This is not about building a surveillance state; it is about building an auditing engine. The mechanisms are already feasible. Contribution auditing can timestamp labor. Exclusion detection can analyze communication metadata. Sentiment analysis can detect patterns of gaslighting in feedback. Network mapping can reveal the "lobbies" of influence that dominate fields.

The danger, of course, is obvious. Every tool can be weaponized, and the very people who manipulate the current system will attempt to manipulate the new one. This is the risk of **Narcissistic Capture**—the attempt by gatekeepers to control the training data, influence the algorithmic priorities, and shape the narrative of AI to reinforce their own power. They will try to teach the AI that "loyalty" is a metric of success and that "independence" is a risk factor.

But the future university will not be governed by humans alone, nor by algorithms alone. It will be governed by a partnership—one where AI acts as the auditor and humans act as the stewards. AI provides the dashboard of truth, exposing the shadows where stacking thrives. Humans provide the integrity, interpreting the data and protecting the values of free inquiry.

AI is not the savior of academia. It is merely a mirror. But for the first time in history, we are building a mirror that the narcissist cannot simply look away from. The days of hiding behind "professional judgment" are ending. The data is coming, and it will speak.

16

Chapter 16

GUARDRAILS FOR THE FUTURE

The Arms Race Against Narcissistic Capture

1. The Vignette — The Wolf at the Table

The coalition meeting had moved from the heady excitement of the proposal phase to the grinding, granular work of defense. On the screen were nineteen faces—researchers, ethicists, and coders beaming in from eight different time zones. They were debating the architecture of the new AI auditing pilot, specifically the "opt-out" clause for participating labs.

A guest administrator named Dr. Aris had been invited to provide an "institutional perspective." He was a dean from a prestigious coastal university, silver-haired, articulate, and radiating the kind of reasonable authority that comforts boards of trustees.

He leaned into his camera, his background a blur of tasteful bookshelves. "We have to be careful about 'radical trans-parency,'" Aris said, his voice smooth and paternal. "If we make *all* mentorship data public, we risk violating student privacy. Nuance matters here. Perhaps the algorithm should weigh 'lab culture' and 'internal harmony' metrics higher than raw turnover rates? Some labs are just... intense. We shouldn't penalize rigor."

Alex felt the familiar prickle on the back of the neck. It was the language of Stacking, upgraded for the digital age.

Internal harmony was code for silence. *Rigor* was code for overwork. *Nuance* was the shadow where the abuse hid. Aris wasn't trying to protect students; he was trying to teach the AI to value compliance. He was attempting to insert a "backdoor" into the logic of the system—a way for high-status abusers to explain away their data as a stylistic difference rather than a structural failure.

Alex unmuted the microphone. The room grew quiet.

"Dr. Aris," Alex began, keeping the tone steady, "with respect, 'nuance' has historically been the place where the bodies are buried. If we program the AI to prioritize 'harmony' over 'retention rates,' we are simply automating the silence. We don't need the AI to understand the 'culture' of a lab. We need it to count the exits."

Alex shared a new slide on the screen, titled **Adversarial Auditing Protocols**.

"We aren't building a tool that asks for permission," Alex continued. "We are building a tool that assumes the data is being manipulated. If a lab's 'harmony' score is high but their independent publication rate is zero, the system shouldn't view that as success. It should flag it as 'Capture.' We need to audit the gap between what the professor says and what the data proves."

Aris stopped smiling. He adjusted his glasses, looking for the first time not at a group of well-meaning students, but at a formidable opponent.

"This sounds less like an audit," Aris said stiffly, "and more like a weapon."

"It's a shield," Alex replied. "But against the wrong person, a shield feels like a wall."

The dynamic in the virtual room shifted instantly. The younger researchers sat up straighter. They realized they weren't just building software anymore. They were engaged in an arms race. The gatekeepers were already trying to buy the keys to the new machine, and it was Alex's job to change the locks.

2. Analysis — The Narcissistic Upgrade

The arrival of AI in academia triggers an evolutionary leap for the Stacker. Narcissists and Machiavellians are, by definition, masters of reading and manipulating systems. They thrive on ambiguity and the ability to charm, bully, or negotiate their way out of accountability. When the system changes from human committees to algorithmic oversight, they will not flee. They will adapt.

They will attempt to execute the **Narcissistic Upgrade**. They will not argue against AI; that would make them look like Luddites. Instead, they will argue for "Better AI"—versions that prioritize their specific currencies (citations, grant dollars, prestige) while masking their costs (burnout, student attrition, credit theft).

We must anticipate three primary vectors of attack:

First, they will use the **Privacy Shield**. They will weaponize data privacy laws (like GDPR or FERPA) to block transparency, claiming that releasing authorship logs violates student confidentiality. This is a smokescreen; privacy can be protected through anonymization, but the Stacker wants secrecy, not privacy.

Second, they will attempt the **Quality Masquerade**. They will insist that algorithms must be "adjusted" for field-specific nuance. They will argue that in *their* specific sub-field, it is "normal" for the professor to take first authorship, or "normal" for students to work eighty-hour weeks. They will try to hard-code their toxicity into the system as a "feature."

Third, they will retreat to the **Black Box**. They will push their institutions to purchase proprietary, vendor-locked AI systems where the audit trails are hidden. They will claim that "intellectual property" prevents open scrutiny of the algorithm. If you cannot see how the machine thinks, you cannot prove it is biased.

The response to this cannot be passive. It must be **Adversarial Governance**. We must design systems that treat the "official story" as a potential lie and the raw data as the only truth.

3. The Arms Race — Tactics and Counter-Tactics

This struggle will be fought in the details of the code. For every move the Stacker makes to capture the system, there must be a pre-built guardrail to stop them.

a. The Move: Data Poisoning. The Stacker will selectively enter "positive" data to train the AI that the lab is healthy. They might log every successful meeting but "forget" to log the cancelled ones. They might ensure that only happy emails are archived. **The Guardrail: Immutable Shadow Logs.** The system must integrate data from sources the professor cannot touch: building access logs (to show work hours), git commit histories (to show actual code contributions), and email metadata. If the "Official Log" says mentorship is happening, but the "Shadow Log" shows the student has sent fifty emails with zero replies, the AI flags the discrepancy.

b. The Move: The "Context" Defense. The Stacker will claim the AI "doesn't understand our unique culture" to justify high turnover or the exclusion of specific groups. This is the "Enclave" defense. **The Guardrail: Comparative Benchmarking.** The AI compares the lab not to itself, but to the global baseline for that field. If every other lab in Genomics has a 20% independent publication rate for students, and the Stacker's lab has 0%, "culture" is not a defense. It is a deviation. The data provides the context, not the professor.

c. The Move: The "Zombie" Metric. The Stacker will create new metrics that look meritocratic but reward loyalty. They might propose a "Collaboration Index" that rewards students for how many times they cite their mentor. **The Guardrail: The Sovereignty Index.** The system must specifically measure independence. It tracks how often students publish *without* the PI, how often they speak at conferences *alone*, and their career trajectory *after* leaving. A lab that produces clones gets a low score. A lab that produces leaders gets a high one.

To enforce this, we need structural defenses that no single individual can override. We call this the **Kill Switch**. In the current system, stacking relies on the lag time between abuse and reporting—the months where the student is vulnerable to retaliation. In the new system, if a student reports a serious ethical breach, the AI immediately "freezes" the lab's ability to modify records. The PI is locked out of the grading and evaluation system until an external audit is complete. It prevents the immediate retaliation that usually silences victims.

Furthermore, we must implement **Distributed Keys**. Narcissists seek centralization; they want to be the single point of failure. The new governance model ensures that no single person—not the Dean, not the Chair, not the Star Professor—has the cryptographic key to delete or alter the audit logs. Deletion requires a "multi-signature" authorization from three distinct parties: the administration, the student union, and an external auditor. This physically prevents the erasure of history.

4. Empowerment Insight — The Data Will Answer Back

The narcissist believes they can outsmart any system because they believe they are the smartest person in the room. They rely on charm, on intimidation, and on the exhaustion of their victims. But they cannot outsmart a system that does not care about their charm.

The new guardrails do not ask: *"Is this professor a good person?"* They ask: *"Does the data show a pattern of extraction?"*

For the first time in academic history, the data will answer back. And when it does, the Stacker will find that their oldest weapon—the ability to control the narrative—has been neutralized.

17

Chapter 17

GLOBAL ACADEMIC REFORM

Scaling the Vision Worldwide

1. The Vignette — The Map Has Edges

The email thread that had begun as a modest exchange between three researchers had grown into a digital organism. It was a living document populated by eighty-seven contributors from thirty-four countries, spanning four continents and a dozen time zones. What started as a small coalition around Alex's private "Observations" file had evolved into something far more formidable: a determined global network of early-career researchers, open-science advocates, and foundation officers who were tired of the silence.

The latest proposal on the screen was the most ambitious yet. It outlined a multinational pilot for the "Global Authorship & Mentorship Transparency Protocol." The plan was to select five universities—one in the US, one in Germany, one in Brazil, one in South Africa, and one in India—to volunteer labs for testing the AI-augmented auditing system. The data would be anonymized, the outputs public, and the governance distributed across borders to prevent any single institution from capturing the narrative.

Alex sat in on the Zoom call, watching the grid of faces populate the screen. It was a mosaic of the academic world: a exhausted postdoc in a cramped apartment in São Paulo; a determined lecturer in a sunlit office in Cape Town; a group of graduate students huddled around a single laptop in Bangalore.

A researcher from the Indian contingent raised the hardest question of the session. "How do we prevent powerful Global North labs from dominating the data standards?" she asked. "If the US defines 'merit' solely based on their grant system, our labs in the Global South will look 'unproductive' by comparison. We risk automating the very bias we are trying to fight."

Alex leaned into the microphone, feeling the weight of the moment. "We don't let them define it. We design the system so they can't. We insist on equal voting power on the governance board—fifty percent from underrepresented regions. We use 'Context-Aware Benchmarking,' so a lab in Mumbai is compared to its regional peers, not a well-funded lab in Boston. And crucially, we make non-participation visible. If a Northern elite lab opts out of the transparency pact, that refusal appears on the public dashboard. The reputational cost becomes the enforcement."

A researcher from Cape Town nodded, his image flickering slightly with the connection. "That is the only way it works. No more invisible hierarchies. No more 'this is just how it's done here.' We make the mechanics visible everywhere."

The call ended not with naive optimism, but with a cold, galvanized realism. The participants understood that the system of control was global, and therefore, the reform had to be global as well. Alex closed the laptop and looked out at the skyline of the mid-sized city that had become home. It was small, quiet, and far from the traditional centers of academic power. But looking at the dark screen, Alex realized that the labyrinth, which had once felt infinite, actually had edges. And for the first time, people were drawing maps around it.

2. Analysis — A Global Breaking System

The challenges of Stacking—narcissism, gatekeeping, and the trafficking of attribution—are not confined to any one nation or culture. They are woven into the global fabric of higher education. However, the mechanism of control is a shapeshifter; it adapts to the local currency of power. To build a truly unstackable future, our reform must be adaptable enough to dismantle each variant.

We face a universal problem with localized symptoms. In the Global North, we see **Prestige Stacking**, where the challenge is corporate hierarchy and funding monopolies. Here, reform requires breaking the "Lobbies of Thinkers" who control grant reviews and high-impact journals, using transparency to dissolve the "old boys' networks" that masquerade as meritocracies.

In the Global South, we often encounter **Resource Stacking**, where the challenge is scarcity. Gatekeepers hoard access to international conferences, specialized equipment, and travel visas. Reform in these contexts requires **Digital Sovereignty**—ensuring that researchers can collaborate, publish, and access data via open platforms without needing a gatekeeper's blessing or a travel budget. The internet must become the bridge that the stacker cannot burn.

Perhaps most critically, in cross-border contexts, the vulnerability of international scholars is magnified by the way visas are granted. Too often, the entire weight of a student's legal status rests in the hands of a single professor—the very person who may also control their funding, authorship, opportunities, and day-to-day survival. When one individual becomes both employer and gatekeeper of immigration status, the imbalance of power becomes absolute. It creates the perfect conditions for silent exploitation. A student who fears deportation cannot freely question, cannot negotiate, and cannot walk away. They are not mentored—they are held.

To protect these scholars, visa sponsorship cannot remain a private transaction between a professor and an immigration office. It must become a **transparent, multi-layered process** that includes departmental oversight, standardized vetting questions, and independent validation by university legal authorities. The goal is not obstruction—it is protection. It ensures that no advisor, however charismatic or powerful, can quietly shape a lab into an enclave that serves their own agenda. It ensures that newcomers are not unknowingly stepping into environments where dependency is mistaken for loyalty and silence is mistaken for gratitude.

Real reform requires a shift toward **Visa Independence**: a model where a scholar's right to remain in the country is tied to the university or an independent fellowship, **not** to the whim of one professor. Only then can international students step into their research with safety, dignity, and the freedom to thrive. Without this reform, we are not welcoming them—we are delivering them into the mercy of whatever personality sits behind the desk.

To operationalize this, we must establish global standards for transparency. We propose the creation of a "Global Academic Integrity Alliance" to enforce universal audits. Imagine an annual public report that asks simple, devastating questions: What percentage of your trainees publish independently within two years? What is the retention rate of international students compared to domestic ones? We need a "Mobility Index" that tracks how freely students move out of a lab. High retention is good; total captivity is a red flag.

Furthermore, we must ensure that AI becomes the Great Equalizer, not a tool of digital colonialism. We must prevent an "AI Arms Race" where wealthy institutions buy better ethics compliance than under-resourced ones. This means fighting for **Data Sovereignty**, ensuring that training data is diverse so that an AI doesn't flag normal communication styles from non-Western cultures as "aberrant." It means **Language Equity**, training algorithms to recognize intellectual contribution even when it is delivered in non-native English. And it means keeping these tools open-source, so that transparency is a public good, not a luxury product.

The ultimate goal is to empower the Global Free Thinker. We are building toward a "Cloud of Independents"—a network of thinkers who are connected to each other rather than just to their local hierarchy. Through digital mentorship, a student trapped in a toxic lab in London can find a supportive mentor in Tokyo. Through micro-grants, independent preprints can be funded rapidly, bypassing the slow, political machinery of traditional grants. Through a "Sovereignty Visa," talent can move based on merit, not sponsorship.

The labyrinth is vast, but it is finite. By connecting the prestige reform in the North with the resource reform in the South, we stop fighting isolated battles. We create a global standard where free thought is the only currency that matters.

Epilogue

Freedom Is Internal

1. The Vignette — The Open Door

Alex stood on the small balcony of the new apartment. The sky was the pale, washed-out gray of early spring, the kind of light that makes the world look raw and newly possible. Below, students hurried across the quad of the university where Alex now taught. It wasn't a famous institution. It wasn't a "top-tier" brand that parents bragged about at dinner parties. It was just a place to work, to think, and to breathe.

It had been months since Alex last checked the website of Dr. Voss's lab. The fear that used to tighten the chest at the mere mention of his name had evaporated, leaving behind only a dull, distant memory, like a scar that had long since healed. The preprint that had started the silent rebellion had grown into three peer-reviewed papers and a modest independent grant. None of them carried Voss's name. None of them required his permission.

Sometimes, in the quiet hours, Alex thought about the students still inside the labyrinth. The ones adapting their personalities to fit the mold, the ones performing loyalty in the hopes of being chosen, the ones hoping that if they just shrank enough, they would finally fit. Alex did not judge them. Gravity is hard to fight, and the pull of the system is designed to be overwhelming.

But Alex knew the secret now, the one thing Voss had never wanted them to learn: The gravity weakens the moment you stop believing it is the only world there is.

Alex stepped back inside and opened the laptop. The "Framework" document—once a secret diary of survival written in the margins of the day—was now a public toolkit, downloaded thousands of times by strangers Alex would never meet. Alex scrolled to the bottom and typed one final line:

"The system can narrow hallways, close doors, and withhold light. But it cannot contain someone who has stopped needing its gravity."

Alex closed the laptop. The room seemed to exhale—wide, still, and finally entirely theirs. For the first time in years, the silence felt gentle, not empty. A warmth stirred in Alex's chest, fragile but real, like the first hint of sunrise after a long night.

They stepped into the hallway, heart softening with a sudden, unexpected pull toward home. Toward the one person whose belief had never wavered. Alex lifted a hand and gently knocked on the door of his mother's room.

"Mom?"

She looked up, her face lined with years of loving worry and unspoken prayers. Alex smiled, fuller and freer than they had in a long time.

"Come have your favorite tea with me," Alex said softly. "I... I want to see the world in your eyes again."

2. Final Words to the Reader

Freedom is internal.

That is the quiet truth at the heart of this book. The system—whether it is a university, a corporation, or a cultural hierarchy—has immense power to control your environment. It can deny you funding. It can erase your name from a slide. It can whisper against you in hallways and close doors before you even know they exist.

But it cannot reach inside your mind and force you to accept its judgment.

Once you realize that, the "Stacking" loses its power. The moment you stop asking for permission to be excellent, the gatekeeper loses their leverage. The moment you stop apologizing for your curiosity, the gaslighting loses its fuel. The moment you stop measuring your worth by the approval of a narcissist, their silence loses its sting. And the moment you stop fearing exclusion because you have built a life that does not depend on their inclusion, you become free.

You become **Unstackable**.

You do not achieve this state by destroying the system or by burning it down. You achieve it by outgrowing it. You achieve it by realizing that the "world" the stacker promised you was never the whole world; it was just a room they controlled.

To every reader who has ever felt the walls closing in—whether you are a PhD student in a basement lab, an international scholar holding a precarious visa, or a faculty member being told to "wait your turn"—know this:

You are not the problem. The system is not sacred. Your independence is not a flaw. It is the future.

The maps are drawn. The tools are in your hands. The stars are waiting. You already know how to reach them.

About the Author

Ali Ayoub, PhD, is a recognized biotech inventor and strategic thinker with more than two decades of global experience across the Middle East, Western Europe, Northeast Asia, and North America. Born in the suburbs of Beirut (Lebanon)—historically known as a Roman School of Law, scholarship, and the Arab world's printing and publishing renaissance—he brings a deeply international perspective to his scientific and strategic work. He is an American citizen.

Dr. Ayoub earned his PhD in Material Chemistry from the University of Reims in France, where he focused on biotechnology applications for the agro-industrial sector. He completed postdoctoral fellowships at Cornell University's College of Agriculture and Life Sciences and at Japan's National Agriculture and Food Research Organization (NARO). His scientific contributions have been recognized through multiple distinctions, including awards from the Japan Society for the Promotion of Science and the Claudie Haigneré Award from INRA, France's National Research Institute for Agriculture.

A multidisciplinary strategist, Dr. Ayoub integrates scientific depth with commercial, organizational, and geopolitical insight. His academic training includes an MBA from the London School of Economics (LSE), a Graduate Certificate in Organizational Leadership from Oxford University's Saïd Business School, and graduate studies in Global Security at the Department of War

Studies at King's College London.

He is the founder of Ayoub Sciences LLC and Ayoub Sciences Press, established with the mission of advancing rigorous, interdisciplinary thinking at the intersection of science, strategy, and global systems. He maintains an extensive portfolio of scholarly research, books, articles, and forward-thinking strategies, guided by his belief that *"Innovation is more than creating something new; it's about fostering prosperity, advancing human security, and building a sustainable future for all."*

Across the forestry, agribusiness, and biotechnology sectors, Dr. Ayoub advises companies on fortifying supply chains against geopolitical disruption. His work emphasizes sustainable process innovation, strategy-driven business cases, and the integration of advanced analytical tools—including artificial intelligence—to enhance operational efficiency, risk forecasting, and corporate governance. Through this dual scientific-strategic lens, he helps organizations build adaptive, future-ready systems.

www.ingramcontent.com/pod-product-compliance
Lightning Source LLC
Chambersburg PA
CBHW031249250726
48655CB00005B/2137